Copyright 2009 Joe Lynch

Published by Woolfee Moon Publishing
Printed and bound by Landor Print Ltd
·wood Road, Garretts Green, Birmingham B33 0TG

ISBN - 978-0-9563394-0-9

000000348692

Frankie sings to little Connie Melland, a local girl at a special
Sunday afternoon matinee at the Dunes Hotel.

FRANKIE VAUGHAN
THE MAN AND HIS MUSIC

By Joe Lynch

DEDICATION

This book is dedicated to our youngest son Simon
who was a kind and talented young man.
He was very much loved by his brothers and his sister
and is missed more than words can say.
We hope that he has found the peace he longed for.
He was the inspiration for the writing of this book.

Tribute to Frankie Vaughan
by his son David

Being the eldest child, I was able to spend quite a lot of time with my father when I was a young boy. After a show and late at night we would travel to the West Country to go fishing. Dad would tell me of big fish deep in the water. I used to think how he was wanted by everyone but he just wanted to be with me. It was fabulous to be with him and I felt very lucky. We had wonderful times together.

As I grew older, I would listen to what he said - "If you contribute something in life, you will always be happy", and I have found this to be very true. I have seen the effects of my father's philosophy in the communities dad worked with.

I am contented with my life and when people have asked why I am so happy, I repeat what my father had told me.

When my father sang to his audience, he sang with his heart, no one used a stage like him. There was no difference between the performer and my father; he was the same person to me, he was just my Dad. He is still very much part of the family.

We miss him very much.

PREFACE

It is ten years since Frankie Vaughan passed away and since then, I have tried unsuccessfully to obtain a biography of his life; apparently, one has not been written to date. The answer was always the same no such book exists. I find this incredible considering his popularity and the huge following by fans all over the world. I have always been a fan of Frank and kept any newspaper articles, and collected his records. My wife Judy and I had been to see him a number of times over the years and always enjoyed the show immensely. He gave a wonderful performance each time we saw him. We also had a very enjoyable time at three of his birthday parties through 'Frank and Friends', his fan club

I have never written a book before and I am sure it was a shock to Judy when, unexpectedly I said I wanted to write this biography. She laughed at me and thought I was joking. I had no idea how I would go about it and ignorance is certainly bliss, if I had known what it entailed it probably would never have got off the ground. I knew I would not be able to do it by myself, as I had never used a typewriter let alone a computer. Fortunately, Judy had worked as an office administrator for a number of years and was able to use a computer but first we had to buy a computer and printer. Judy was a little sceptical at first as she had been retired for a number of years and was pretty rusty. Still nothing ventured …

When the computer was installed and up and running, we began with the material we had at hand. I then asked for a letter to be printed on the letters page of the Birmingham Evening Mail requesting any memories of Frank and possibly photographs. He had many fans in the Midlands, especially Birmingham. Within a couple of days, the letters stated to arrive, some included photographs. I also had a number of telephone calls. Everyone wanted to talk of his or her memories of Frank.

I also contacted a good friend of mine Barbara Lees, who had been a fan of Frank's for years, and was a member of his fan club. She had carrier bags full of memorabilia of all kinds, and said I was welcome to take them away and go through them, to keep them as long as necessary.

I then had a letter followed by a telephone call from Pat Hassell. Pat and her late husband Ralph had been very good friends of Frank and Stella. Pat informed me that she had a Red Book of memorabilia and I was welcome to go through it at her house. She did not want me to take it away as it was very dear to her. I was not sure what I would find but Judy and I went to see Pat and her daughter Michelle and we were made very welcome. Before we left we felt like old friends. Pat was now quite happy to let us borrow her book, which was a folder of about four inches in thickness, packed with information, photographs and a number of telegrams. These all provided us with a wonderful insight into their friendship with Frank's family, which covered many years.

The afternoon ended with Pat sitting at her piano playing a number of Frank's songs. We thoroughly enjoyed our time with Pat and Michelle, and felt like old friends as we left with the promise to return Pat's collection as soon as possible. From then on there was no stopping us. This book is the outcome of everyone's kindness and enthusiasm for a wonderful entertainer who was a much loved and highly respected man.

ACKNOWLEDGEMENTS

My thanks go to Stella Vaughan for giving her blessing to this biography of Frank's life. Stella has been very encouraging from the start, for which I am most grateful.

I wish to thank my friend Barbara Lees for allowing me to use the wonderful collection of memorabilia covering Frank's life, which was a great help in writing this book.

In addition, sincere thanks to Pat Hassell for allowing the use of her 'Red Book' with so many details not widely available, lovely photographs and telegrams. It has been a pleasure to read, with information which would have been impossible to obtain without Pat's kindness.

My thanks to Author Spencer Leigh offered much needed guidance from the very beginning.

My thanks go to Vince Hill, Marty Wilde and Tom O'Connor for their lovely written memories. They did not hesitate to pay tribute to Frankie Vaughan when approached. In addition, to Jimmy Tarbuck who telephoned his tribute to Frank. They had been very good friends for many years.

To the staff in the archive department of Liverpool library for their infinite patience and time they spent photocopying many old newspaper articles.

To all the fans in the Midlands for their telephone calls and written memories of Frank, he would have loved each and everyone.

To Ronnie Quinn from Glasgow for the information on Easterhouse, and his life in and around Glasgow as a young man in the 1950s. Also, his meeting with Frank regarding Easterhouse.

Grateful thanks to them all.

CHAPTER 1

I decided to write this biography of Frankie Vaughan's life for two reasons; I had admired him over the years not only as a performer but for his dedication to his fans, and for the vast amount of money he raised for different charities. Yet no biography has been written of his life in the ten years since his passing.

When I called upon him for help to raise money for a charity for the mentally ill, he did not hesitate to agree to give   his   support. However, unforeseen circumstances arose which made it impossible for him to fulfil his promise, but more about that later.

The happenings of one particular day can change everything about ones life. The day which changed the life of my family, was a beautiful warm summer day in June 1991. My wife Judy and I went to collect our youngest son Simon, who lived in a flat in Edgbaston, which is on the outskirts of Birmingham city centre. We had visited him the day before and he was looking forward to coming with us the following day, Sunday to visit his brother Mark, who lived in Evesham, Worcestershire. He and Simon had always been very close and had a lot in common.

When we arrived, I remained in the car while Judy went to tell Simon we were ready for the journey. When Judy had no response from Simon, she   felt immediately that something was wrong. She decided to use the spare key Simon kept in case he locked himself out. When entering the flat, Judy found Simon in bed. At first, she thought he was still sleeping, but soon realised he was dead. She was panic stricken and ran down the stairs to where I was waiting. I immediately called an ambulance, even though in your mind you know there is nothing they can do. It was later found that he had taken an overdose of prescription and non-prescription medication. Simon had suffered from schizophrenia since his late teens. The medication for schizophrenia can have very disturbing side effects. One of the most upsetting consequences of this was taking away Simon's personality and inducing almost permanent lethargy. He had very little pleasure from life anymore.

Simon was twenty-six years old; he was a gifted artist and had attended art college, a very kind and quiet young man. He always had many friends both at college and at home. He was very much loved by his older brothers and sister. The pain of our loss was unbearable for all the family, and we found it almost impossible to cope with losing a much loved son and brother. However, eventually we all had to go back to work and try to carry on with our lives. This was the hardest thing to do but we had to get on with everyday life to the best of our ability.

A few months after losing Simon, my brother asked if we would like to buy tickets for a charity dance, which was to raise money for a lady who had lost her husband. We really did not feel up to socialising at all but were finally persuaded to go out for the evening. The music that night was an Irish Show Band called "Claddah" headed by an old friend of mine, Tom Kelly. His band played all over England and Ireland. It was lovely to see Tom after quite a number of years. My brother had told him about the loss of our son, he was very upset and offered his condolences. Tom told me to give him a call if there was anything he could do to help.

After a while, I decided that I would like to do something to raise money for an organisation, which helped people with all kinds of mental illness. Simon had been in touch with The National Schizophrenia Fellowship and they had been very kind to him. Simon had only a small amount of savings but we donated it to the NSF and they bought a computer and printer with the money.

I telephoned Tom Kelly and asked if he and his band would be prepared to play at a charity show. He immediately agreed to play at a local dance if I could arrange one. This I did at a very nice club in the City of Coventry, which is not far from where we live. Tom was true to his word, he and his fellow players accepted no payment whatsoever. We raised £400 and once again donated it to the NSF. I organised a variety show at the same club with a number of local talent. The star of the show was the comedian Ken Goodwin.

I wanted to arrange a show, which would raise a large amount of money to help an organisation, which supported the mentally ill. I had no idea how to go about it and found the thought quite daunting. In addition, whom would I ask for help? Unexpectedly Judy said, "Why not ask Frankie Vaughan?" We had been fans of his for a number of years and were familiar with his charity work. He was a very popular star and much liked by everyone who knew him. I felt he would be the perfect choice. From quite humble beginnings, he had achieved so much during his lifetime with hard work and determination. After much thought I decided to give it a try.

There is no doubt that Frankie Vaughan became an international star and his fan club spread as far as South Africa, America and Australia. He earned a great deal of money and raised millions of pounds for different charities. However, his parents had a hard time in Liverpool and struggled to bring up their family but young Frank had a very happy childhood.

CHAPTER 2

Frank Ephraim Ableson was born on February 3 1928 at Liverpool Maternity Hospital. Liverpool is located in the north west of England. It is a very industrial City as well as a busy shipping port. When Frank was born, the family lived at 135 Kirkdale Road, almost opposite the Rotunda Theatre, which opened in the 1860's but was destroyed in the blitz during the war.

From Kirkdale Road his family moved to number 37 Devon Street, which is close to the London Road, and this leads down to Liverpool's famous Empire Theatre near to the City centre. When the family later moved to the Lodge Lane area, they were only round the corner from the Pavilion Variety Theatre, known locally as 'The Pivvy'. It seemed he was never far from a theatre even in those days!

He was eventually joined by three young sisters Myra, Phyllis and Carole. The rest of the family consisted of his mother, Leah, and father Isaac and his grandmother Freda. Frank would become known to the world of show business as Frankie Vaughan. Due to one of his most popular songs, he later became known affectionately as 'Mr Moonlight'.

Frank's grandfather Ableson, left Lithuania when he was 16 years old. He and his friend, George Hackenschmidt, travelled together. They both had a love of sport and wrestled their way through Europe, and eventually made their way to South Africa, where they worked in the diamond mines. George later became a world famous wrestler. Frank's grandfather gave up wrestling professionally in his early twenties, but throughout his life he did exercise to keep in good physical condition. Frank put his own love of sport down to his grandfather.

However, grandfather Ableson was also a cultured man who spoke four or five European languages. Because of his fluent Dutch, he served as an interpreter with the British Army in the Boer War. His services won him the right to come to Britain. Eventually he married in his early thirties and he and his wife settled at Edge Hill. There Frank's father was born.

Frank's maternal grandmother, Freda Kozak, came to Liverpool from Kiev, Russia when she was only 21. She had her two very young children, Frank's mother and his uncle, and just a bundle of clothes. We have to wonder how anyone managed to survive that kind of journey in those primitive days, especially a woman with two young children. Freda must have been a very strong and determined lady. Her maiden name was originally Cossack. Frank said that in adversity she had the courage of the Cossacks! That she was dark, gay and lovely and had many admirers, even offers of marriage. She turned them all down and dedicated her life to looking after her children and grandchildren.

Her husband had gone to visit relatives in a distant part of Russia, he never returned. At first, the family thought he had been caught up in one of the programs, frequent in pre-Revolutionary Russia - and had been murdered by the Cossacks. They later learned that he had gone off by himself to America to avoid service in the Imperial Russian Army.

Many years later, when he travelled to the United States of America, Frank had been able to find the city in America where his grandfather had settled. A number of times when he was appearing in America, he had the urge to try to trace him and his possible descendants. However, Frank felt these things are sometimes better left alone.

Since his father, an upholsterer, and mother, a seamstress, both worked long hours, it was Frank's grandmother Kozak, who took care of him. She took him all over Merseyside, The Pier Head, where the ships docked, and to New Brighton. They would take crusts to feed the pigeons.

In the dock area, Frank always loved the big shire horses pulling the carts. Because he spent so much time with his Grannie, as he always called her, he of course, thought the world of her. When the great Atlantic liners came in he used to clutch his Grannie's hand, as they seemed so big to a little boy. She entertained him with stories about Russia, about the time she and her family had lived there.

At the docks when the big carthorses passed, Grandma Freda would tell him that in Russia, they used to breed horses and she would go to them and whisper in the horse's ear. Sometimes it would whinny, as if it understood what she was saying. Frank was convinced she had some special power that could make animals understand her. She would lift Frank on to a horse and they would smile and wave to the friendly Dockers. They would finish their visit with tea and great big Eccles cakes at the Pier Head coffee stall.

All these tales fired his imagination and he was determined to travel when he was older. As his life turned out, he did an enormous amount of travelling during his career.

When Grannie took him to New Brighton, he loved the freedom of the sand, and having a ride on the fun fair. She taught him to catch crabs, and how to hold them without being bitten. He used to take them home in a bucket.

On one occasion, Grannie did not want him to take them home, but he won. On the Mersey ship going back home, they were on the top deck. Frank lost his balance, the bucket was tipped, and the water and the crabs fell on the passengers below.

When he was older, no matter how hard up the family, his Grannie would always find a few pennies so that he could go out with his chums. He used to enjoy visiting museums to see the gallery of shipping, showing the evolution of merchant vessels from earliest times. On Sundays Frank and his pals used to tour Liverpool by tram for a penny, including the Pier Head and the parks.

For a time, before he even went to school, he was a bit of a young rogue. A gang who took things from market stalls befriended little Frank, and one day the older boys made him their look out for the 'coppers'. He was only a little boy, not yet at school, but he would shout to the rest of the gang when he saw a policeman coming. Unfortunately, he was the only one who was caught. The policeman, who was a kindly Irish man, took him along to Grannie for a real ticking off. As he was so young the ticking off was all he was dealt.

CHAPTER 3

When he reached school age, his grandmother took him along to his first school, Harrison Jones School. The first day at school terrified him. He had not been at school long when a teacher discovered that he had some talent in drawing. When she told the whole class how good he was, he could feel himself going red in the face. He was a very shy child and tried to stay in the background. One boy called him a 'cissy' and the whole incident made him feel he was the odd boy out in the class. He cried himself to sleep that night and wished the teacher had not singled him out in the class.

As he grew a little older, he and his pals liked playing on the cast iron shore at Dingle, an area on the edge of the Mersey. This was a rather grim stretch of the Mersey Banks at the south end of the City of Liverpool. The cast iron shore was named such because of the local foundries, and the red iron ore that ran down onto the beach.

The swimming baths in Tunnel Road was another enjoyable pastime for the youngsters. In addition, they would walk round Aintree racecourse the day before the Grand National. Saturday afternoons were spent at Paddy's Market or the match at Anfield. These were all simple pastimes, but as money was very short in those days, youngsters found a lot of pleasure in these activities.
Frank wanted to be a Boy Scout, but his family could not afford the uniform. Other poor boys used to attack the Scouts in envy. Because of this experience, as he grew up, he began to dislike uniforms, however good the cause. He did not believe in any boys brigades, whatever their denomination. This was why he was so in favour of the boys' clubs, they have a no uniform rule.

When he was eight years old, Frank's father, Isaac, took an upholsterers shop on the corner of Lodge Lane. The family moved to 45 Eversley Street, near Granby Street, where Frank then went to school, and he was chosen to sing in the school choir. It was while at Granby Street that he first started to show a talent for art. He would copy photographs from the papers - including one of Adolph Hitler. At first, nobody would believe that he had done them. It was even worse when they did believe him, then they would call him names.

Years later, Frank was to learn that one of the girls, who also attended Granby Street school, grew up to be a well-known singer. She was Lita Roza who was born in Liverpool March 1953. Lita became a very popular singer with the renowned Ted Heath Band along with Dickie Valentine, another singer of the day who, over the next few years, became a very good friend of Frankie Vaughan. Lita reached the top of the hit parade and was the fist ever Liverpool artiste to have a number one record. The song was 'How Much is That Doggie in the Window?' She hated the song, but was persuaded to record it by her agent. Although she never did sing it again, she made a lot of money from the sales which enabled her to buy her first house.

In 2001, Lita was invited back to her home town of Liverpool to open the 'Wall of Fame' on Mathew Street opposite the Cavern Club. Hers was the first in a series of wall mounted bronze discs that celebrate over fifty number one records from Liverpool stars including Frankie Vaughan and The Beatles. More recently, Atomic Kitten was added to the line up. Sadly, Lita Roza died in August 2008.

When he was nine, Frank was transferred to another school near Liverpool's Philharmonic Hall. The hall is now one of Liverpool's great venues for concerts and includes a unique Walturdaw rising cinema screen, the only working screen of its type left in the world.

The original Hall was built in 1849, and has long been an acclaimed and integral part of the cultural life of Liverpool, and was described as the 'best in Europe' by Sir Thomas Beecham before being dramatically destroyed by fire in 1933.

The present hall was designed by architect Herbert Rowse and opened in

1939. It has continued its established reputation as one of the UK's premier arts and entertainment venues, as both a concert hall and cinema. The art deco splendour of Liverpool Philharmonic Hall was restored in 1995 following a £10.3 million refurbishment; parts of the foyer are said to be based on decoration in the tomb of Tutankhamun.

One day, all the children were singing in class when the headmaster, Mr Levy, asked Frank to go out to the front to him. Mr Levy said he liked Frank's voice, as it was deeper than the other boys. He soon became a member of the choir at Princess Road Synagogue, which was one of the most magnificent in Britain. His payment was 12s.6p for three months, but sometimes he managed to earn another few shillings at another synagogue. This was big money in those days to a young boy. He still did a lot of drawing, but he was also good at sports. One day he won the 100 yards, 200 yards and the three-legged race in one afternoon.

The Jewish faith was important to Frank from a child. Judaism is very much a family faith and the ceremonies start early, when a Jewish boy baby is circumcised at eight days old. When a boy reaches the age of 13, he has his Bar Mitzvah. This is a ceremony marking the fact that the boy has achieved this age and is consequently obliged to observe the commandments.

The belief is that a Jew is someone who is the child of a Jewish mother; although some groups also accept children of Jewish fathers as Jews. Someone who is not born a Jew can convert to Judaism, but it is not easy to do so. Judaism means living the faith, it is a faith of action and Jews believe people should be judged not so much by the intellectual content of their beliefs, but by the way they live their faith - by how much they contribute to the overall holiness of the world.

Many Jewish religious customs revolve around the home. One example is the Sabbath meal, when families join together to welcome in the special day. Frank would not accept work on Jewish religious days. He and the family always celebrated such days together as a family. Jews observe the Sabbath, the Jewish holy day, and keep its laws and customs. They often call the day Shabbat, which is Hebrew for Sabbath, and which comes from the Hebrew word for rest. The Sabbath begins at nightfall on Friday and lasts until nightfall on Saturday. It actually starts a few minutes before sunset on Friday and runs until an hour after sunset on Saturday, so in actual fact it lasts about twenty five hours.

All through his life, Frank tried to live a good life not just within his family but in everything, he did. When he did finally make it in show business, and needed an accountant and solicitor to look after his interests, he chose to give the work to two of his old school pals who had chosen these particular careers.

CHAPTER 4

By the time war was declared in 1939, Frank's father had managed to save enough money to allow them to move to a house in Smithdown Lane. He also bought a shop, where being an upholsterer, he renovated and sold old furniture.

At school, everyone knew that Frank liked to sing and when the air raid sirens went and the boys trooped into the shelter, the other boys would ask Frank to give them a song. He would only sing if every single light was switched off. Then, in complete darkness, he would get up and sing 'I Don't Want To Set The World On Fire'. Very appropriate with bombs dropping all around!

Of course Liverpool was very badly damage during the war, and at times, it seemed that the Germans were throwing everything they had just at Liverpool. However, all the bombing did not deter Grannie, who still lived in Devon Street, which luckily had not been damaged by the raids. She preferred to be with the family during air raids, and would walk to Smithdown Lane just to be with them all. Once she took shelter in the Majestic Cinema which is on the London Road, even though the cinema had been machine-gunned a short time before.

One day the sirens wailed as usual and all the family hurried down to the shelter, which was at the end of the road. Bombs were falling thick and fast, and they heard an extra loud bang. The family emerged from the shelter and rushed down the road only to find their new home had been bombed. It was a heap of rubble.

Frank was evacuated to Endmoor, near Kendal, in Westmorland. When he was 13, the whole family was reunited at Lancaster where Frank went to the Lancaster Boys' National School. Here he had a lot of encouragement in his art studies from one of the teachers, Mr Barrow. He studied the work of Van Gough and, in his inexperienced way, would try to copy his technique. When he could, he would go to the art galleries and have a look around on his own.

Years later, while discussing his childhood, Frank confessed that when at the Lancaster Boys' National School, he was pleased that he was Jewish. This meant that he did not have to attend religious instruction, as the other pupils had to do. It also meant he could fill the time running around the playground and kicking football.

Frank was now 14 years old, when one day he got into a fight with another boy at school. They both gave as good as they got, but a teacher saw what was going on and gave them a good telling off. He then packed them off to the nearest boys club saying, "It will do you much more good than behaving like a hooligan, and they'll teach you to fight properly".

The club leaders taught the boys a lot, which included being involved in sport. One sport they taught the boys was boxing, which Frank loved. In fact, they did a great deal for all the boys by keeping them interested in worthwhile activities, and guiding them in the direction to suit their talents. Frank later realised how much the club had done for him, and it was a pity that so many other youngsters did not get a chance to join one. He also realised that the club encouraged everyone, no one cared what religion or nationality you were. There was no division or discrimination of "class, creed or colour". A boy was just another boy and he was judged only by his behaviour and by the kind of person he was.

By now he had realised that running with a gang was not for him, and would only lead young people into trouble. He never changed his mind about this, and of course he later gave so much to the Boys' Clubs in the hope that it would keep some of the youngest on the straight and narrow.

Leaving school at the age of 14 going on 15, Frank had no idea what he wanted to do in life. He was encouraged to use his art ability, which was very impressive for such a young lad. Two years ahead of the age normally expected, he passed the thesis on the subject of the Liver Building. This won him a scholarship to Lancaster School of Art. Not many youngsters of his age managed to win a scholarship especially as far back as the 1940s.

Without the scholarship, there would have been no way his family could have afforded to send Frank to College. There was not enough money to stretch to this in such times of hardship. While there, a lovely man named Mr Grimshaw came into Frank's life. He spent time with Frank and was very encouraging as he saw the potential in him. As he was at college virtually on trial, he knew he had to work hard and do his very best. The patience and encouragement of Mr Grimshaw eventually paid off!

By now, he was a real fan of the Boys' Clubs. He captained the soccer team at centre forward, ran an art class, and did a bit of singing. He was accepted by Lancashire and Cheshire Federation of Boys' Clubs soccer eleven, and took a youth leader's course. He got talked into singing in a club concert party - mainly on the strength of his previous choir work. In this show he gave his rendition of 'Old Father Thames' and some hilly-billy songs. Anything to do with art, sport of even singing was alright with him.

As he had been bought up with three sisters, Frank was not so keen on bothering with girls yet. However, he did have one experience when, on his way home from art class, he noticed a young girl eyeing him. She was very pretty and other boys seemed to be interested in her and try to make a date with her but she ignored them. She called him over, and asked if he would take her to the pictures that afternoon. He was a little worried and quite embarrassed but flattered. He was not going to miss an opportunity like that so off they went to the pictures.

They were watching the film for a while, when Frank had a shock. Somewhere a few rows behind them, he could hear people talking very softly. Although they were talking very low, they were unmistakably the voices of his grandmother, mother and sisters. He panicked. He was supposed to be at school. He sank down into his seat, and then slid down to the floor. He then crawled out on his hands and knees, and went hurrying back to school. Needless to say, the girl did not ask him out again.

CHAPTER 5

During the second world war, Frank's father had joined the Pioneer Corps where he eventually rose to the rank of Sergeant Major, and took part in the D-Day landings, but by 1945, he had been invalided out of the armed forces. He was unable to do any heavy or strenuous work; therefore, Frank would do what he could to earn a few shillings to help.

The following year Frank had his call up papers for the army to say he was to be conscripted. However, this was deferred for a year to enable him to take an art examination. Conscription, which was sometimes called the draft or National Service, was when young men of 17-18 years of age were compulsorily called to serve for one to two years in the armed forces, but it could also be for an indefinite time if it was a time of war.

Frank did not actually hear that he had passed his examination at the College of Art for which he was deferred, until his father wrote to tell him. This meant that when he came out of the Army, he could become an art teacher, if he decided to do so.

By then he had been to Ireland, Aldershot, Malta, and then Egypt with the Royal Army Medical Corps. He quite liked the Army, and enjoyed the travelling. In fact, he volunteered for a posting as medical orderly on Corvettes, which is a lightly armed warship for escorts and anti submarine duties, in the Mediterranean. This is when he had an opportunity to sing.

Frank spent six months in Malta, and became very fond of this lovely sun-drenched country. Every café had a band, and every radio played Neapolitan love songs, but he noticed they were not very good at the top songs of that time. It occurred to him that he might earn some extra money by trying the clubs for some work. He did an audition with bandleader Paul Arnaud, at the Café Premier. He was in luck; they took him on to sing at night when he would be paid twenty-five shillings each night. He had a whale of a time every evening and got paid for it! Frank could not believe that he was being paid to do something what he would do for free, he loved singing so much. He even picked up some of the Maltese language, and a little Italian.

Home on leave just before his demob in 1949 and coming up to his twenty first birthday, something happened which knocked him for six. He met his future wife. Living round the corner from the Ableson family, was a tailor who had four daughters. Myra had become good friends with the tailor's eldest daughter Stella. She was a little older than Myra.

While Frank had been away in the Army his sisters had grown up. Myra was almost 18, although he found it hard to believe. To him she was still his baby sister. When she said she was going off to the Mecca ballroom with a girl friend, and asked him if he would like to go along, he was shocked. He told her she was much too young to go to those places even though her parents were happy for her to go. He was certainly playing the older brother and she found his presence a nuisance, after all he had been away a long time and Myra was used to going to dances with her friend Stella. She was determined to go to the Locarno dance hall as she had agreed to meet her friend there.

Frank went out for the evening with the lads to the local cinema but unfortunately, there was a long queue and eventually they were told it was a full house. They did not want to go to the pub for a drink and just did not know what to do. Eventually they decided to carry on to the Locarno dance hall where he knew Myra would be. Frank was determined to keep an eye on her. The Locarno, had a name for trouble on occasion, and he was taking no chances. He wanted to make sure that Myra was safe. He soon spotted his sister; she saw him at the same time and hid behind the girl she was with. As Frank approached them, the girl turned round and laughed, knowing that he was going to give her a piece of his mind for encouraging his young sister to go to the dance hall. However, when he saw Myra's friend he forgot his sister completely, he was so taken with her. She introduced herself as Stella Shock.

Frank wanted to make a good impression on this lovely girl who had bowled him over. He was well known for being a bit of a singer, he also knew the bandleader, Harry Gray, who asked Frank if he would like to do a song. He jumped at the chance to impress Stella and jumped up on stage. He thought Stella was beautiful with deep-set dark eyes, and a beautiful flashing smile. He asked her if she cared to dance. Stella nodded and smiled. Later, he could not even remember what they had talked about.

At the end of the evening, Stella agreed when Frank asked if he could walk her home. When they arrived at Stella's home, they made a date to meet again. He had fallen head over heels in love with Stella. Frank asked her if she would be his steady girl friend, and of course she accepted. This was the boy who did not have anything to do with girls but he certainly had been smitten. What would the lads say about it?

Their first date went quite well, and Stella's mother made him very welcome with tea and cake. They sat and listened to records on a wind up gramophone. From then on, they saw each other as much as possible. Later in life, when being interviewed he said, he was not a man who could have affairs, as he would not like to get involved in such dangerous games.

Stella was working in a chemist's shop, and studying pharmacy at night school. Frank asked her if she would be his steady girlfriend, he was well and truly in love with this lovely young woman and was ecstatic when she agreed to his request. Fifteen months later, she and Frank became engaged and married soon afterwards on 6 of June 1951 at Francis Street Synagogue. They spent their honeymoon in Devon. Frank was still studying for a long time after he met Stella. They wanted to spend as much time as possible with each other and this meant that Stella had little time for her studies to qualify as a pharmacist. Eventually, she gave up her studies.

Later when Frank was starting to make his name in show business, he was told to keep Stella in the background, and not to mention her at all and the fact that he was married. It was thought his fans would not like the fact that he was a married man. Well, he did not like it one little bit, but he agreed. Stella was the big secret of his life, until their first child was born.

As he now had the qualification, he did consider teaching art, but the money was not too good. He thought he would have a better future in commercial art. His grandmother still saw him as a potential show business star, rather than a serious art student. She was convinced that he would end up on the stage. However, fate was to intervene.

CHAPTER 6

Every year in Leeds, the students held a Rag Week, the highlight being a Rag Revue. It was a very popular show and in 1950, as there was so much talent around, the organizers decided to hold it at the huge Empire Theatre. Frank was a great hit performing in the revue doing a medley of Al Jolson songs. Al was a Lithuanian-born American entertainer, vaudeville performer, actor and singer.

He was born Asa Yoelson, May 26 1886 in Srednike, Lithuania. His family settled in America where his father worked as a cantor in a synagogue. Al also had a love of singing, but he did not want to sing in the synagogue. Instead, he and his brother Harry sang on street corners to earn money. Al then discovered he really enjoyed performing.

He and his bother eventually teamed up to play vaudeville in New York, but he much preferred to work alone therefore, he and Harry decided to go their separate ways. Al spent several years playing small clubs in California. He wanted to have an act that was a little bit different to the normal singer. He decided to black his face and sing in a Southern accent. His popularity grew and his songs, such a 'Sonny Boy' Swanee' and 'My Mammy' were song by his audience long after they had left the theatre. He became very well known for this type of song. He would go down on one knee when singing 'Mammy' and pretended to cry to his mother, saying he would "walk a million miles" for one of her smiles. Jolson died October 23 1950 in San Francisco, California.

Although Frank sang a number of these sentimental songs, which Jolson used to sing, he did not "black up" and try to impersonate Jolson. He liked the songs which happened to be associated with Jolson. After the show, Stanley Joseph, the son of the then manager of Leeds City Varieties, came to speak to him. He gave Frank a letter from Barney Colehan the entertainment producer, and told him that if he ever considered going on the stage professionally, to take the letter to the Bernard Delfont Agency. He took the letter, and kept it in case he ever had the chance to use it. He was not too impressed with the idea though, he knew what a tough life show business was. At that time, he still liked the idea of becoming a commercial artist. But he was talked into giving an audition for band-leader Harry Parry, a fine clarinettist. Harry was most helpful and gave Frank a try-out in Leeds for ten pounds. He later offered Frank a long-term contract, which he turned down as he felt there would be no future in it.

A Yorkshire furniture firm, exhibiting at Earls Court, London, wanted a display idea for their stand. He entered the competition, and won. The first prize was 30 guineas for two weeks' work designing stands. It was a lot of money in those days and winning Frank confidence and made him feel very hopeful, but unfortunately, no more work came his way. He still was not sure what to do but show business was not on his mind. Although a cousin of his Bill Ableson, was doing his best to encourage Frank in this direction.

Frank entered a Hughie Green 'Opportunity Knocks' radio show. These shows were to look out for fresh talent and Hughie Green hosted the show. He was later compere of this same show when it was transferred to television on the ITV network in the mid - 1960s. He first became a household name in the 1950's with the ITV quiz show, Double Your Money.

When Frank went along for audition, Hughie said it was fine but he had no room in the next show for a solo singer. So Frank teamed up with a good girl singer called Irene Griffin, who was also trying her luck on the show. They travelled to London for the finals and just missed winning. They came second. In a way, he was pleased they had not won as he certainly did not want to be part of a double act.

Frank and Stella were renting a flat in Macclesfield Street, Soho, but money was a very big worry for them with no work on offer. By now, they found that Stella was expecting a baby. It was very hard to keep the fact from the landlord, as he did not like tenants either with or expecting a child. In fact, Stella had to buy a larger coat to conceal the fact of her pregnancy.

CHAPTER 7

None of the agencies was interested in his art and Frank began to think that he had nothing to lose by having a go at singing. He still had the letter of introduction he had been given and decided to present himself at the Delfont Agency in Haymarket. He handed the letter to a girl on reception who told him to wait. A few minutes later, she came back to tell him that Mr Billy Marsh, Mr Delfont's representative, was very busy and could not see him at the moment. Frank decided to hang around for a while in the hope that he would eventually be seen.

On his way out for coffee, he bumped into such well known performers as Elsie and Doris Waters, Jimmy Wheeler and Max Bacon. All were celebrities of the day.

He went back to the office and waited until it was being closed for the night. Then an office boy, a youngster of about 16, came out. Clearly his job was to get rid of Frank. They chatted for a while and Frank learned that his name was Leslie Conn. Later in life he became an executive in a music-publishing business and would always plug any song released by Frank.

As a last resort, Frank asked Leslie if he would take the letter in for him. All he wanted was for someone to open his letter. The lad was now coming round to Frank's side and was quite sympathetic. He took the letter into the office. Then a slightly-build man came to the door and asked Frank why he was in such a rush. Frank told him he wanted to see Billy Marsh. "I'm Billy Marsh, what's your hurry?" Frank just about got his words out when he said "I want to sing".

Billy Marsh, who was a well-known agent in show business, took Frank into his office. Marsh asked if he was any good at singing, and Frank, trying to sound more confident than he felt, said, "Yes, I'm very good". Marsh asked Frank what he had been doing and he said "Stands" Marsh said "One-night stands, where?" to which Frank answered "No, exhibition stands". Marsh looked puzzled and said, "Well I can't listen to you here. Tell you what, get yourself a pianist and a rehearsal room and I'll come and hear you sing". Frank had just two pence which he used to telephone a friend who loaned him ten pounds to pay for the room and pianist. The room was at Mac's opposite the Windmill Theatre. When he had rehearsed, he went back to Billy Marsh's office.

Another agent was sitting in the office along with Billy Marsh. He said to Frank "I'll give you some good advice son, remember until you hold it in your hand, you have nothing". He always remembered that advice. Frank sang two songs for them, 'Powder Your Face With Sunshine' and 'Pennies From Heaven'. They were quite impressed, and agreed to give him a chance. He was not offered any money, not even pennies, but he was offered a ten minute spot at the Kingston Empire on the following Monday, without pay. If he clicked he could do the week. If not, Billy would probably never see him again. Billy said "Do well, boy, and we'll talk money".

Frank went out the next day and hired a pianist, Julian Oakley, and promised him ten pounds for the week, whatever happened. He was taking a real chance because he did not have even ten shillings let alone ten pounds, but he had to take a chance and give it a try. They rehearsed all the week-end and got together a few songs.

Nobody at home knew he was going to do the show, not even Stella. He was supposed to rehearse at 11 a.m. but he was running late, nobody had told him how far it was from the West End. Luckily, Julian had got there on time and had persuaded the producer to wait for Frank.

Waiting in his dressing room that night, he was very nervous. He was in such a state, he was sure he would not remember a word when he got on stage, and wondered if he stood any chance of getting the next train home. Comedian, Jimmy Wheeler, was top of the bill. When he went on stage and introduced Frank, he told the audience, "This is a new boy having his first break. Sit back and enjoy yourselves" and he beckoned Frank on to the stage.
Frank was so nervous, he was convinced that he would forget the words to all the songs. He could see nothing of the audience due to the lighting.

He decided to give it all he had and hope the audience liked him. He sang 'Powder Your Face With Sunshine'. When he finished singing, he could not see anything, as the footlights were so bright. It seemed at first there was no one there. Suddenly he heard a muffled roar. He could not understand what it was until he realised it was applause and cheers. He just about managed quite an awkward bow.

This great reception gave him confidence, and he thought that maybe he had a chance of some success after all. He did five more numbers, one after the other, and the audience shouted for more! He could not do any more as he had run out of music.

When he went back to the dressing room, the manager told him he had telephoned Billy Marsh. He said Bernard Delfont was coming with him to the theatre, and were bringing the press. They shook hands, and as he wandered out, the manager shouted, "You close the first half, next house. The number two spot".

The next day Billy told Frank, "You did very well son, so pack your bags at the end of the week. You top the bill at the Hulme Hippodrome, Manchester". When Frank made no comment, Billy said "You don't sound very enthusiastic". Frank replied "I'm wondering what I'm gong to do about food. Is this another of those no-salary jobs?" Billy laughed, "You get paid all right. One hundred pound a week".

The show was called 'The Old and The New'. Also in the show was male impersonator Hetty King, she came to congratulate him. Over the years, Hetty became a great help to Frank as she had years of experience before her.

Hetty was born Winifred Emms on April 4 1883 in Shoreditch, London. She adopted the name Hetty King when she fist appeared on the stage of the Shoreditch Theatre at the age of six with her father, William Emms (1856-1954). Emms was a comedian who used the stage name Will King.

By 1905, Hetty was appearing in music halls, with her solo act, as a male impersonator, often dressed as a "swell" in top hat and tails. Her career spanned both world wars when she performed in uniform of either a soldier or a sailor. She also played the "principal boy" in many pantomimes. She continued to entertain until the end of her life, touring with the show 'Thanks for the Memory'. She was cremated at Golders Green Crematorium.

After the show at the Empire, Jimmy Wheeler threw a party for Frank at his Battersea home. Frank always looked upon Jimmy Wheeler as his lucky mascot. Jimmy had helped him a lot on that opening night. They met again two years later. Frank was down on his luck at that time, but it changed overnight and he landed a gramophone company audition. He also met Jimmy again in 1955, and afterwards he was immediately signed for an ice show called 'Wildfire'. It seemed that every time he met up with Jimmy, his luck changed for the better. When they met up again in 1956, within a few days Frank was signed to do a big summer season at Blackpool.

On May 25 1956, Stella gave birth to their daughter, Susan. Stella and Frank were overjoyed to have a second child. Frank took the baby for a stroll in her pram along the front at Blackpool when he was appearing there. When he was spotted by some fans Frank stopped to talk to them, and they were delighted to have a peep at the new baby.

When the Duke of Gloucester was speaking at the inauguration of National Boys' Club week he mentioned Frank. He said, "Christopher Chataway, Roger Bannister (both athletes) and Frankie Vaughan are showing a fine lead to other young men in their twenties. All three are playing their part in helping the Boys' Club movement". Years later, Frank was to say that this had been one of the proudest moments of his life.

CHAPTER 8

After the Kingston Empire opening night, Frank was signed up by Billy Marsh and Bernard Delfont to top the bill at Manchester for £100 a week. He couldn't believe he was to be paid this amount of money. It was a fortune for him and he thought of what he and Stella could do with so much money. He still had not told the family about the show, as he thought they would not believe him. He was unaware that they had read stories about him in the morning papers, and Stella and the family all turned up to see him. They sat in the stalls on the Thursday evening, clapping like mad when he came on.

Still Billy Marsh was not satisfied as he did not like Frank's surname. He said Ableson would not click with the crowds, it just did not sound right for a singer. He asked the surname of Frank's grandmother. When Frank told him Kozak, Billy thought that was even worse. They looked through the telephone directory, trying to find a name more suitable, but nothing seemed right. Frank decided to telephone his grandmother for help. She was a little upset to think that he was not going to keep his own name but took the news calmly. "You always be may number vorn grandson Frank". 'Vorn' soon became 'Vaughan'. That was it. From then on Frank Ableson was known as Frankie Vaughan.

He noted all that took place on stage, and learned a great deal about show business from this experience. Hetty King once told Frank that a star should enter and leave the stage door looking like a star. She also told him never to go on stage in a lounge suit. She recommended a self-tied bow tie and a black suit from a top tailor, even if he could not afford them! Later in his career, his public became used to him always looking immaculate, and he would not have it any other way. He was very particular about his shoes. He said if his shoes were right his balance was right and he walked correctly which made him feel good.

Both Stella and Frank thought that he was on his way to the top, but it was not that easy for him. If he had not had the advance of the hundred pounds from Billy Marsh, he would not have been able to pay his pianist or his fares. Just when he was again beginning to worry about money, he was offered a couple of Northern Region broadcasts for the BBC, which was arranged from Manchester. He thought things were beginning to look better. However, the broadcasts did not turn out as well as expected. After all, recording was very new to him and he felt he was too raw. Mainly because of this, his first record for Decca, did not turn out too well.

He went on touring, topping the bill at places like Workington, Barnsley and Leeds City of Varieties. He learned a great deal from Hetty King and Winifred Atwell. Winifred was a very accomplished and versatile pianist who was very popular in Britain throughout the 1950s. She was born in Trinidad 27 February 1914 and came to Britain with her family.

She had studied the piano since she was a small child. By the late 1940s she had gained a place at London's Royal Academy of Music with ambitions of becoming a concert pianist. However, in order to finance this, she worked during the evenings at London's clubs playing jazzy piano rags.

By 1950, her popularity had spread nationally and she began recording with Decca during 1951 - before record sales charts began. She also appeared on television where she made regular appearances. Her rendition of 'Black And White Rag' was one of her most successful numbers. It has been used as the signature tune of BBC's 'Pot Black' snooker programme. Winifred continued to give well-attended concerts until her retirement in 1978. She died during 1983.

Jack Jackson was also touring with Frank, but he did not really get to know Jack until they took part in a charity show to help the dependants of those men killed in the Creswell Colliery disaster. Jack told Frank that if he made any more records in future to send him a copy. He thought he could possibly help him.

Jack Jackson was a bandleader and trumpeter born in Barnsley, Yorkshire, 20 February 1906. He started playing the cornet at 11 years of age in local brass band contests, but began his dance band career playing violin and cello in 1922 when he was just 16. He was the son of a brass bandsman and conductor.

Jack was taught to play the trumpet by a man named John Solomon at the Royal Academy of music and subsequently worked in circuses, revues, ballrooms and on ocean liners. In August 1927, Jack got his big break with Jack Hylton's band. He played many fine solos whilst with Hylton and also sang on occasion, generally using the latest modern "scat" techniques.

He was with Hylton for over two Years, leaving in November 1929 to join Howard Jacobs band at the Berkeley Hotel, then to The Savoy Hotel. In August 1933, Jack Jackson opened at the Dorchester hotel with his own band. He became immensely popular with the smart set at the Dorchester and the band was always popular with the dancers.

In December 1939, he moved to Rector's Club, then to the Mayfair Hotel in March 1940. During the war, he spent some years at the Ministry of Information drawing cartoons. He also worked as a band booker at Foster's Agency, but he was not cut out to work behind a desk, and he missed the band. He made a comeback with a new band at Churchill's in February 1947, opposite Edmundo Ross. Ross's orchestra played lively Latin dance music and was very popular at that time.

Jack Jackson eventually gave up band leading to compare a BBC big band series called "Band Parade". The following year he was given his own late night record show called "Record Round Up". This was in June 1948 and it ran for over 20 years making him a household name all over again with a new generation and an audience of 12 million.

Jack died in Rickmansworth, England, January 1978, just short of his seventy second birthday.

While in the north of England, Frank made a small television appearance. He felt it was not very good, but he thought his grandmother would be the happiest old lady in the country when she saw him on screen. It was only what she had planned for her grandson. He was finally on 'the movies' and a vast audience would be seeing him too.

Sadly, Frank's grandmother did not live to see his career take off, as she passed away in 1950 at the age of 65 years. Of course, her death was a great blow to all the family, but especially to Frank. She had played such an important part in his early life and instilled in him true values, which he never forgot. She was very much missed by them all.

CHAPTER 9

For the following eighteen months, Frank had very little work, except for odd jobs singing with local bands. He did not seem to be having any luck with the Decca label, his records were not selling too well, he therefore decided to try a different label. By now he was becoming quite concerned, and decided to go round all the record companies hoping that he could obtain a record contract. He visited ten in all but it was only when he got to HMV, the very last one, that he had any luck at all. This is where he first met Wally Ridley.

Wally was one of Britain's best known record producers. In the late forties he joined EMI Records as a producer for the HMV label and went on to sign a whole range of up and coming singers such as Alma Cogan, Donald Peers, Anne Shelton and Ronnie Hilton, as well as the bandleader Joe Loss and the comedian Benny Hill.

Wally was responsible for guiding the early career of Vera Lynn and it was his personal decision that EMI should acquire for UK release Elvis Presley's Heartbreak Hotel from RCA Records in the USA. He was also a prolific songwriter - he wrote more than 200 songs and numbered among his compositions 'I'm in Love for the Very First Time'. During the war, he worked closely with Vera Lynn, the much loved forces sweetheart, coaching her and accompanying her on all her radio and theatre engagements. He was also responsible for her recording 'We'll Meet Again' which was to become her signature tune. It was very nostalgic for our men fighting overseas. Wally also found the song 'Bring Me Sunshine' for Morecambe and Wise.

In 1977 Wally Ridley retired - the same year that HMV ceased to exist as a recording label - but he still produced albums occasionally. During his long career he won two Ivor Novello Awards for his contribution to the music industry. Wally died on January 23 2007, aged 93.

When Wally first met Frank he asked why he looked so worried. Frank explained the situation with Stella and himself, and that there was a baby expected. Wally said he would hear Frank sing. He sat at the piano and played whilst Frank sang "My Sweetie Went Away". Ridley obviously was very impressed with his singing, as he agreed to give Frank the much-needed contract. He got no money from his first sessions and had to wait for the royalties to come in. They were just one penny per record, but he had a contract at last.

He and Stella were listening to the radio one evening and Stella said how wonderful it would be if "My Sweetie Went Away" was on the radio. They then heard Jack Jackson introducing "Record Roundup" and there was Frank's record being played on Jack's programme. Jack gave it a big build up and Sam Costa, another radio disc jockey, who called Frank "Smiling Boy", played it on Housewives' Choice. It was also played on Radio Luxembourg, which helped a lot.

Another record followed soon after and the interest created brought Frank to the notice of Val Parnell. This resulted in him being signed up to top the bill for a tour of the Moss Empire circuit.

Val Parnell was a theatre and music hall impresario, and television executive. He was born in London on Valentine's day in 1892. He was christened Valentine Charles Parnell but known simply as Val. By 1945 he had become Managing Director of the Moss Empire music hall circuit, in charge of some of London's most prestigious theatres.

In 1956, he was appointed Managing Director of Associated Television and presented Val Parnell's 'Sunday Night at the London Palladium' until 1965. He resigned his position at ATV in 1962 to make way for Lew Grade and retired in 1966. He died 22 September 1972.

CHAPTER 10

After struggling financially since they had married, Frank and Stella now found that they were in a position to rent a flat in Hamilton Terrace, St John's Wood. From that time, Frank's career went from strength to strength. His first hit record was in January 1953 with the song "Istanbul" (Not Constantinople). This was a cover version of a very popular song originally released by "The Four Lads" a Canadian group. They originated in Toronto where they were very popular in their own country, and several covers were performed by such artists as Caterina Valente 1954 and Bette Midler in 1977.

On the day Stella expected David he opened in variety as top of the bill at Leeds Empire. It was his first big number one date and the same theatre where he had appeared in the University rag. He worried himself into a terrible state thinking about Stella and the baby. He found it hard to think of anything else.

This went on all week and David did not arrive until the following Monday October 1953. Frank was appearing in Birmingham and that night he gave one of his best performances, his first as a father.

When Frank did the show in Leeds the previous week, the audience got very excited over his performance. The fans went mad outside the stage door, he and Bert Waller, who had recently become Frank's accompanist, were unable to leave the theatre for nearly an hour. Bert Waller had been accompanist to Gracie Fields and Frank considered himself very fortunate to have such a fine player and felt the success of his tour was thanks, in no small measure to Bert's experience and ability. Gracie had been singer and comedienne who was well known for her theme song, Sally, and had song to the troops in world war II.
The girls got so excited they broke in through the front of the theatre and kept up a chant of "We want Frankie". In the end, the police had to smuggle him out of a side entrance. Still the youngsters tried to force the windows of the car. In the end, Frank and Bert managed to escape to safety. Frank said of this kind of situation "It can be a little daunting at times but when they get excited and surge forward to try to talk to me, I really do not mind. I feel the attention is quite flattering to me as an artist".

Among the presents his fans have given him over the years have been rosaries and religious paintings and he treasured them all. He tried never to let his fans down for he felt that they had shown such tremendous loyalty to him, and where would any performer be without their audience?

CHAPTER 11

After Leeds, life became hectic once again and he had little time to himself as his work included a great deal of travelling.

Bert Waller became his bosom pal, they played golf together; in fact, they went everywhere together and Bert taught Frank a great deal about presentation. For the first few weeks of that big tour, Bert would watch Frank for hours as he practised such little things as walking on and off stage. All the fans loved Bert and got to know him pretty well.

As much as Frank loved the theatres and performing, he never lost his love of sport. He was determined to keep as fit as possible for his variety act. To perform so many performances required a lot of stamina, which meant he needed to keep in shape Some of the football clubs allowed him to train with them when he was appearing locally.

One time, he went to join the Barnsley footballers at a training session. He turned up bright and early and put on his tracksuit. The players seemed friendly enough but what he did not know was that they had decided to try to run him off his feet.

They all started lapping the ground at a leisurely pace, but gradually it quickened. He then got the idea that they were trying to make him look a bit soft. He never did like to give in or being beaten even into second place. So he gritted his teeth and kept going. Round and round that track they went, with Frank feeling more and more tired and feeling that his legs would soon give under him. The players kept looking at him as if expecting him to collapse at any time but in the end, Frank won. The players stopped before he did and, grudgingly, they accepted that he had beaten them at their own game.

That night he was in agony. Every bit of his body ached. He even thought he would have to sing sitting down for the duration of his act, but he did manage to drag himself on stage. Then, before he even managed to sing a note, an ear-splitting cheer came from the front of the theatre, the entire Barnsley club had turned up to give him a big reception at the show.

From then on, he made friends with many sportsmen up and down the country - with great football stars like John Charles, Duncan Edwards and Ronnie Allen.

John Charles - was born in Wales December 27 1931 and christened William John Charles. He played centre half and centre forward for Leeds United, Juventus, Roma, Cardiff City, Hereford United and Merthyr Tydfil. He was also player/manager for Hereford and Merthyr Tydfil. He was awarded a CBE in 2001. He died February 21 2004.

Duncan Edwards - was born in Dudley, England on 1 October 1936. He played Wing Half for Manchester United. He was one of the Busby Babes, the young United team formed under manager Matt Busby in the mid 1950s, and one of eight players involved in the Munich air disaster. Edwards survived the crash of the team's aeroplane at Munich in February 1958, but died as a result of his injuries 15 days later.

Ronnie Allen - was born on 15 January 1929 in Fenton, Stoke on Trent, England. He played for Port Vale, West Bromwhich Albion, and Crystal Palace. He played for the England National team 1953 - 1954 and managed Wolverhampton Wanderers, Athletic Bilbeo, Sporting Lisbon, Walsall, West Bromwich, Panathinaikos FC and back to West Bromwich Albion 1981-1982. He died on 9 June 2001 at the age of 72.

Ronnie and Frank were very alike to look at and had occasionally even been mistaken for each other. Both he and Ronnie played soccer in the same position (centre forward). When West Bromwich Albion won the Football Association Cup, Frank was every bit as pleased as the players. One evening at the theatre, Ronnie, Ray Barlow and a gang of the team brought round the Cup for Frank to have a look at. I wonder if this could have been the first time the trophy had ever been back stage at a theatre?

It was during this major tour that he decided to set aside some weeks so that he could tour Boys' Clubs. Some people in show business thought that this was just a 'gimmick' to gain popularity. Frank was annoyed when he heard this and insisted that he really got a kick out of going round and meeting the lads in these clubs. Of course, it was through clubs such as these that he was taught to have a true slant on life after his experiences as a youngster. It truly meant a lot to him.

When the National Association of Boys Clubs (NABC) first heard of his interest, they asked him to organise a national talent competition among their 166,000 members and he felt very honoured when they called it the Frankie Vaughan Talent Competition. He thoroughly enjoyed himself and it seemed everyone else did too.

CHAPTER 12

Over the next couple of years, Frank found he was so busy it was difficult to find time to get away on holiday with Stella. He was engaged to play a romantic singing role but was also expected to skate. It was in a big ice show, called "Wildfire", at the Empress Hall, Earls Court, London in 1955. He was the first singer to play a part in this kind of show with a microphone strapped to his chest. He started practising skating weeks before the show was to open. He was quite keen on skating and used to roller skate when he was a youngster. Of course balance is everything when skating on ice and his precious skating experience did help a little with his ice skating.

He decided that if he and Stella did not take a few days holiday at that time, then it would be impossible once he started the show. They went away for a couple of weeks at Bournemouth. He knew that it could be a long time before he was able to take Stella away again.

Frank was warned by his skating instructor that he must practise every morning. No sooner had he and Stella arrived in Bournemouth than he had a call from the BBC to do a rush broadcast during the first week of their holiday. That was a couple of days out of their first week away.

Frank then had a call from Billy Marsh saying he was short of a 'top of the bill' for the New Royal Theatre at Bournemouth the following week. Billy said it would be nice and handy for Frank!

The second week of the holiday included skating practice and topping the bill - with a very small amount of holidaymaking during the afternoon.

Frank found "Wildfire" a great experience. There was a slight problem when the mike broke down and he could only be heard by a few people in the vast arena but in the main, it went without a hitch. He was so pleased that he did not fall over once while he skated. It was only when he decided to walk on for the finale wearing his shoes that he came a cropper!

One evening when he had gone in among the audience to sing, one person sitting ringside flung her arms round him and greeted him. It was Lady Docker! She was a very well known and flamboyant personality, the wife of Lord Bernard Docker who was Chairman of BSA Motorcycles until 1951. Frank was probably very surprised to see her at the ice show.

On tour Frank always took a pair of dumb-bells around with him for some extra training in his dressing room. Sometimes he even had full weight-lifting classes organised in the theatres.

He was performing at Bradford and Bert really had to play the body-guard. The dressing rooms were below street level and they could hear the fans outside getting more and more excited. Somehow they managed to make their way inside and he heard a little tap on the door.

Frank and Bert thought it was one of the theatre staff, he had stripped off and had only a towel round his middle, but Frank called "Come in". Within seconds, the dressing room was crammed with near hysterical girls who found that the only souvenir to grab was his towel.

Frank hollered to Bert "Get me out of this, Bert or we are going to find ourselves in a scandal". The only way Bert saved the situation was by throwing his weight about a bit, but he did get the dressing room cleared and Frank's modesty was saved!

In 1955, Frank awarded and presented the annual "Frankie Vaughan Trophy" to the Brady Ramblers who were the Brady Boys Club's Hebrew folk music group. When funds were needed to be raised for the Ramblers to tour Israel, Frank joined singer Alma Cogan, and actor David Kossoff, in an evening of song and laughter.

CHAPTER 13

Frank's record "Green Door" was released in November 1956 and reached number two in the hit parade. The high kick which Frank did whenever he sang 'Green Door' on stage, came about when he requested the brass section to play a little louder when the words 'Green Door' were sung. It was suggested by Francis Essex that he kick his leg whenever he wanted them to play louder. He thought it was a little silly, but the producer said he should keep it in the act. From then on it was always associated with Frank, and that particular song.

One day when finding his way around Glasgow, he took a walk down the famous Sauchiehall Street. Whilst looking in a music shop window, he noticed some of his sheet music displayed there. He went inside to thank them for displaying his music, as any advertising helped promote him, and it never hurt to thank people. Whilst browsing, he saw a very old music sheet with the picture of a woman on the cover. She had her hair tied up in a bun, her name was Nora Bayes who was a vocalist born in 1880. In the early nineteen hundreds she was known for a number of songs including 'Shine On Harvest Moon,' and 'Has Anybody Here Seen Kelly.' She was a headliner in vaudeville through the mid 1920s but died in Brooklyn in 1928.

The song that Frank found with Nora's photograph on the cover was 'Give Me The Moonlight, Give Me The Boy, and Leave The Rest To Me'. When Frank asked how much the music sheet was he was told one shilling and sixpence. This turned out to be the best one and sixpence he had ever spent. He took the music sheet back to the theatre to run through it with the piano player, and the rhythm section. An idea had occurred to him when he first read the words. He was looking for something, which would instantly be associated with Frankie Vaughan.

He decided to change the words to "Give Me The Moonlight, Give Me The Girl and Leave The Rest To Me". For a bit of fun, he decided to use a top hat and cane to go with this new song. He thought it would be a bit of fun and the audience might see it that way too. It actually worked.

He borrowed a top hat from a local funeral parlour and someone kindly loaned him a cane to complete the effect. This was later replaced by his own silver topped cane which he continued to use throughout his career. He had in mind to do an act like Hetty King; use the old soft shoe routine he had learned to do in his act. It seemed to work, so Frank tried it out on the show that evening. When he got to the part, "If there is anyone in doubt who would like to try me out", and all the girls shouted, "try me hen", even the lads were laughing. Frank could not believe his luck; he had found a song that gave him his own personal image for one shilling and sixpence.

From that time on, Frank became known as "Mr Moonlight" for the rest of his life. The top hat and cane became his trademark.

CHAPTER 14

January 1957, 'Garden of Eden' hit the number one spot in the charts. It kept this position for four weeks. The song caused quite a stir and the BBC wanted to ban it being played on air. Some church leaders called it blasphemous as the words suggested that man found it impossible to resist temptation. It still sold a great number of records.

That October he had another hit with "Man on Fire", which proved how popular he was continuing to be. He also made a long-playing record with songs from his films.

From now on Frank was never short of work. For nine weeks, he was top of the bill on the national circuit of Empire Theatres. This included his home town of Liverpool, in May. In the same year, he was presented with the Silver Heart from the Variety Club of Great Britain when he was voted Show Business Personality of the Year.

Sadly, this was the year Bert Waller had to leave Frank, as he had to look after his wife, who had become ill. Bert had been Frank's accompanist for three and a half years. Frank knew he would miss him very much as they had become friends as well as work colleagues, but Bert had to look after his wife. Frank was due to go out on tour and he knew it would be difficult to get along without him but they stayed closely associated and never lost touch.

Another associate was Alan Marriott, of Billericay, who started one of the first Frankie Vaughan fan clubs and eventually became national secretary.

A number of people were recommended to him to take over from Bert, but somehow, they did not quite seem to fit in. Then one day in Liverpool along came Ray Long. When Ray walked in, Frank wondered what was happening, for Ray arrived with his right hand completely swathed in bandages. However, they talked for a while and among other things, Ray told him that he had been Musical Director of the Lyceum Theatre, Sheffield, and played for Hetty King, and Randolph Sutton. He had also been an army officer, a builder's labourer, a seaman and a church organist!

They also found that their entertainment careers had a similar beginning. Frank's at Leeds University Rag Show and Ray's as Musical Director of the Aberdeen University Rag. What impressed Frank most was Ray's sense of humour. He thought that anyone who turned up for an audition as a pianist with his hand bandaged as Ray had done, must have a great sense of fun.

From then on Frank and Ray travelled thousands of miles and performed in many countries. They seemed to have the same likes and dislikes and both had the same sense of humour and are able to see the funny side when things seemed not to be going exactly right. Their families became friends and their wives would get together when Frank and Ray were away on tour.

October that year was David's fourth birthday. Frank had bought him a special present. This was a "Mazel", the Star of David, on a gold chain to wear round his neck. It is the equivalent of a Christian cross. All the family had one and Frank wore his all the time as he felt it had bought him luck.

CHAPTER 15

Frank's records started to sell quite well, and his name was now known in the world of music. This enabled him to get work in a number of theatres, including The Glasgow Empire.

1958 was a special year for Frank. He was selected for a Royal Command Performance at the Alhambra Theatre, Glasgow. There was also a season at London Palace Theatre, which broke all records. He was selected 'Britain's Top Vocal Personality of the Year' for which he was presented with a Silver Rose Bowl, by the New Musical Express. He was also voted 'Top Singer in Films' and topped two sections in the New Musical Express popularity poll.

Frank started a variety tour for Harold Fielding who became one of Britain's top theatrical producers. He produced 'Half a Sixpence' and 'Charlie Girl' among others. Also American imports such as 'Mame', 'Barnum' and 'Sweet Charity'. Frank's variety tour began at the Town Hall, Birmingham on Saturday night. The audience were wonderful and it looked good for the tour.

During an interval between houses, Frank popped round to the Hippodrome Theatre where an old friend, Bruce Forsyth was topping the bill. Frank walked on stage in the middle of Bruce's act, much to Bruce's surprise, and the delight of the audience. Bruce returned the compliment by invading the stage at the Town Hall at the end of Frank's second performance.

From Birmingham, he continued his journey to Manchester for a Sunday concert at Belle Vue. In the audience were Frank's mother, father, and several of his old friends. After the show, he met up with an old friend Lonsdale Bonner and went to stay the night at Lonsdale's home. He had met him when he studied at Lancaster Collage of Art. Lonsdale was now an art teacher in Bolton.

The next morning he was off again and on his way through the Lake District to Glasgow. It was a good opportunity to enjoyed the journey and take in the wonderful fresh air of the Lakes. He received a terrific reception in Glasgow, a sign of his popularity in Scotland. He also managed to spend a short time at the wedding reception of another of his old friends before going on to St Andrews hall for two concerts.

The next stop was Dundee. His first job there was to have tea with 17 year-old Margaret Smith, who had won a competition to become the Scottish Daily Record's "Cinderella Girl". Margaret was selected from thousands of girls for the title. She had been the breadwinner for her family since the death of her father. Apart from having tea with Frank, part of her prize was a front row seat at his concert.

Frank also had another surprise for Margaret, which neither she nor the newspapers had any idea about. He invited her to fly back to London at the end of the tour to spend the weekend with his family. This was a real surprise and Margaret could hardly believe it as it was the first time she had left Scotland and her first flight in a plane.

The tour had finished in Edinburgh the next day.

Marylin and Frankie take time out from filming to pose for this happy photograph.

Frankie has long been an admirer of the talent of Michel Legrand, that fine young French musical director and was delighted to have him on his last recording session.

Frankie is presented to the Queen Mother at the showing of "The Horse's Mouth"

Frankie and Bruce together again at another opening, this time at the hairdressing salon of their friend Gay Bucceri, in London.

Off to catch the 'Happy Train'... could be, but we are inclined to think that Frankie's jumping for joy with success of his show at Dundee.

Lord Althrop presented a gold Keystone to Frankie at 'Clubs are Trumps' night at the Festival Hall to celebrate the sale of 1,000,000 records for the Boys' Clubs.

Just what I'd like...... is that what Frankie's thinking or what David's thoughts are?
Although Susan looks as if she'd rather enjoy playing trains.
This was the Vaughan family at the Meccano Model Exhibition in London.

Hands across the sea. One of the many visitors back stage at he Dunes was Frankie Laine.
Here he is with Frankie, Ray Long and road manager Glyn Jones.

A picture we are proud to print, Frankie with Stella, David, Susan and Mrs Vaughan at the Investiture in Buckingham Palace.

Happy smiles from Stella and Frankie as they arrive at the Carlton Cinema, Haymarket for the Midnight Premiere of "Let's Make Love".

Just a few more minutes to go before their spot in the show - Frankie and musical director Basil Tait put the final touches to their appearance.

Fank with Sammy Davis, Jun.

"Hello Dolly"

If Frankie looks like a King on a Golden throne here, then that bemused smile must be because he can scarcely believe that his "Tower of Strength" is currently reigning at No. 1 in the Hit Parade.

One of the friends Frankie met on his visit to New York was Perry Como. Thay are seen here in the television studios before Perry's show.

Frankie is now appearing permanently in London .... at Madame Tussaud's Exhibition!

During his stay at New York's Copacabana Club Frankie was visited by boxer Ingemar Johanssen just after the latter had won the Heavyweight title crown in the world championship fight with Floyd Paterson at Madison Square Gardens.

CHAPTER 16

Near the end of 1958, Frank started his first continental tour - first stop Cologne, Germany. From the airport, he was driven straight to the studios to rehearse a programme, which was to be recorded later that evening. It would be heard by the British Forces in Germany. The following day he went to Dusseldorf, where he was scheduled to give more concerts to the Forces. During that first week, he and Raymond Long, travelled hundreds of miles through the Ruhr Valley, just giving concerts in the evenings and travelling by car, bus, train and plane during day.

The following Saturday, they were in Copenhagen, Denmark. Frank had been invited to take part, along with a host of famous European artistes, in a Christmas charity concert held every year for the orphans of Denmark. The welcome in Denmark was fabulous. The Danes were very kind people and hospitable to Frank and his party, and they made a great fuss of him.

After various other engagements, which all went wonderfully well, they finally returned to Germany. Frank was guest star on Caterina Valente's Television show in Stuttgart. It was here that something strange happened. Many miles away, in Karlsruhe, a man and his wife were watching their television that evening and when Frank appeared on screen and began to sing 'Give Me The Moonlight', the man could not believe his eyes.

When the programme had finished, he telephoned the TV studio and managed to speak to Frank. He asked if that was Frankie Vaughan speaking. "Yes" said Frank. "You look exactly like the Frank who was such a wonderful friend to me when I was prisoner of war in Egypt twelve years ago. I could never forget that man". Frank was overwhelmed by the call and the two arranged to meet. Kaporal Hermann Schmeiser, late of the Afrika Korps, and Corporal Frank Ableson, late of the British Army, renewed a twelve year old acquaintance.

Very soon, Frank and his team had to leave Germany again for their last stop, Amsterdam. Here they spent three days sightseeing, before Frank appeared in a Christmas week Television Show at Hilversum. Everywhere they had been, people had heard of Frank and wanted to see him. The reaction was terrific, and he had many invitations to return. It certainly had been a wonderful and worthwhile journey, but now it was time to return home.

Frank then started a summer season for ten weeks. This was at the Brighton Hippodrome, and with a man who would become a life long friend. That man was none other than Tommy Cooper. Tommy had become a dear friend of Frank over the years and he was looking forward to working with him once again. Tommy was a much loved very tall 6 feet 4 inches - very clever conjuror as well as comedian. During his act, he pretended to be a bumbling performer with an ability to perform tricks but in fact he was a member of The Magic Circle, an association of very clever conjurors.

He once was a former resident of the Windmill Theatre who came into show business a few months after leaving the army. He mainly concentrated on cabaret work. Whilst at the Windmill, he doubled in cabaret and in one week, he actually performed 52 shows. He also made a trip to America in 1954 to appear in cabaret in Las Vegas. He appeared in four Royal Command Shows - three in London and one in Glasgow. In April 1984, Tommy collapsed from a heart attack in front of the audience and millions of television viewers. |He was midway through his act on the London Weekend Television variety show 'Live From Her Majesty's'. Most of the audience thought it was part of his act and were laughing, until it became apparent he was seriously ill. Unfortunately, he was found to have died when examined by paramedics.

Later that same year, Frank made a move into British films. It was a spoof western with comedy legend, Arthur Askey. The film was 'Ramsbottom Rides Again'. It was the start of several films he would make in the next few years. Whilst making the film he was advised that a song he was due to record in 24 hours time was not suitable. This caused a real panic. Bert and the rest of the team connected with the record were dashing around trying to find an alternative number. Frank popped home to change his clothes. As he pulled a tie out of the drawer, he came across a bit of manuscript paper. It was a song Bert had handed him a long time before which had been forgotten about.

He hummed it through and thought it was pretty good and would be fine to replace the song which had to be discarded. When he got back to Bert and the team, Bert rushed in with a great wad of songs he had picked up around town. He was totally taken aback when Frank said, "It's ok Bert, I've got just the song I'm looking for. It's one of yours". The song was "This is the Night". Once again Bert had come up trumps as he usually did when a song was needed to fit a particular part.

Frank went on to do a season at the London Palladium which he loved. He always felt that the Palladium had a magic all of its own. On the bill with Frank were The Kaye Sister, the King Brothers and Joe Church who were all old friends of his. It was produced by Robert Nesbitt.

Frank had just made a new record with the Kaye Sisters, it was called 'Come Softly'. Since making 'You've Gotta Have Something In the Bank, Frank', he had been hoping to find another song to record with the Kaye Sisters and he felt that this was perfect.

CHAPTER 17

In June 1959 in the presence of the Duke and Duchess of Gloucester, the premiere of Frank's new film "The Heart of a Man" opened at the Odeon, Marble Arch. It was written by Pamela Bower and directed by Herbert Wilcox. Frank played the part of an out of work sailor named Bud. The cast also included actress Anne Haywood, Tony Britton and Anthony Newley. All proceeds would go to the National Association of Boys' Clubs.

Later that year, he made a trip to the United States of America for a tour. He was to appear at New York's Copacabana and would have quite a long run at The Dunes. Frank was in fact the first British singer to appear in Las Vegas, which was quite a compliment to him.

When they arrived, the temperature was still over 100 degrees even though it was evening, and dark. A brand new white open top car was waiting for him and he was driven to the luxurious Dunes Hotel, which was to be his home for the next nine weeks. He and his team received a wonderful welcome from everyone.

He had no sooner arrived at the hotel after eighteen hours flying - than he was told, they would be flying over Hollywood the next day for a stars' party. The party specially given by Arlene Dahl and her husband, Fernando Lamas, at the Beverley Hills Hotel in Frank's honour.

James Mason and his wife Pamela Kellino were there. Richard Burton, Jack Benny, Fabian, Bob Cummings, Robert Stack, famous Hollywood columnists Hedda Hopper and Louella Parson, bandleader Percy Faith and a score of other famous personalities, all waiting to meet Frank.

When he opened his season at the Dunes in September, he had an audience of hundreds of American holidaymakers, journalists, TV commentators and a host of new friends. It was a great beginning to a wonderful season.

As the word went round that Frank was there, more and more people came to see him. His performances received great revues and all were unanimous in their prophecy that one day very soon Frankie Vaughan would be as well loved in America as he was in Britain.

He made a guest appearance on both The Ed Sullivan Show, and Bot Hope Show. Frank caused a laugh when he forgot Hope's name. Bob said, "My name is Bob or Mr Hope". The press in Las Vegas had nothing but praise for Frank and they made such comments as:

Saturated with show biz savvy ...
Forrest Duke, Variety Daily.

Delighting the Las Vegas audiences ...
Louella Parsons, New York Journal-American

Combination of Victor Mature, Frank Sinatra, Dean and Tony Martin
Les Devor, Las Vegas Review-Journal.

England's answer to Frank Sinatra .....the best thing to come out of the British isles in the past 50 yeas...
Ralph Pearl, Las Vegas Sun

A vivid personality and good voice...
Hollywood Reporter

(could) become a top personality in the U.S.
Los Angeles Times

Although he was inundated with appearances, Frank still took the time to speak at the American Boys Clubs convention.

With this amount of engagements to carry out, Frank was away from home a great deal of that year. He missed his family very much and managed to nip over from New York to appear in the 'Sunday Night at the Palladium' TV show in November. He had to be back in New York the following day. The trip across the Atlantic took on 5 hours 50 minutes. The only snag was that England was fog bound and the plane had to land at Prestwick in Scotland. This meant it was 15 hours later before he arrived home. Therefore he had very little time with his family in London. He had a wonderful welcome from them all. At that time they had not seen him for two and a half months.

When he returned to New York after his visit home, he went into the recording studio to make a new record. The titles were "The Very, Very Young" and "If You Fall In Love". It was released in Britain in the following January.

When he finally arrived back in Britain, Frank decided to established a scholarship for "a deserving member of the U.S. Boys' Clubs who exhibits real talent as a vocalist." The winner would be selected from the 600,000 members of American boys' clubs by a panel of expert judges. He would then arrange to have the winner flown to Britain from the boy's home in the U.S. to appear as a vocalist on the annual variety show at the Royal Festival Hall in London for Boys' Club Week, in October. The winning boy would spend three weeks in Britain, with all his expenses paid including spending-money. He would also tour the whole country with Frank, entertaining boys' clubs everywhere. It was a very popular idea by all concerned.

CHAPTER 18

When Frank returned to Britain, it was to a great reception, and he was as popular as ever. He was in great demand, appearing in cabaret, and theatres all over England. In the audience of one of his shows were Anna Neagle and her husband Herbert Wilcox. They were impressed with his personality, and they both thought he would possibly be right for the part in a film they were considering. He was invited along for a couple of film tests.

These tests were both thorough and exhaustive but Anna and her husband thought he was a very natural actor. When the tests were finished, they were both convinced he would be ideal for the part they had in mind. This was to be Anna Neagle's first independent production. However, Anna and Herbert had been a team for a number of years and he was to be the Director.

Frank decided to accept their offer as it was a good opportunity for him, and gave him the chance to prove that he could act. The female lead was played by a young actress, Carol Lesley. Frank put everything he could into the film and in fact, it became The Royal Film of the Year.

This film was called "These Dangerous Years". It was a dramatic story of the 'dangerous years' between leaving school and forces call-up set against a tough, realistic background of the Liverpool water front and army life. Frank was making his first appearance on the screen. He portrayed Dave Wyman, leader of a gang known as the Dingle Boys, who rebels against civil and army authority.

It also involved dealing with Teddy Boy gangs and the problem of adolescence, this film offered a wonderful start to his acting career. He had some doubts about whether he could handle such an important role, but both Anna Neagle and Herbert Wilcox were very reassuring.

Because the film was set in Liverpool, the local residents were very interested in all that was going on and could be seen at every location. Naturally, Frank was the main attraction and the fans would follow him at every opportunity. They were never told where the next scene was to be photographed, but one way or another they found out and there they all were again. Within a few short minutes of the unit setting up 'camp', hundreds of people were there watching, waiting, commenting, with pencils and paper ready for the chance of an autograph.

Frank was given a lot of help by everyone at the studios, which gave him more confidence, and he then found that he enjoyed the work immensely. On his first day of filming, he ran into the actor Richard Todd, who was making 'Yangtse Incident'. When Richard showed him the 'rushes' of a four-minute scene where he was in close up all the time, Frank was struck by the fact that he hardly ever blinked his eyelids. Richard told him that on screen, everything is magnified. A blink in the wrong place can distract an audience. That was his first real acting lesson. The location work being on his own ground, so to speak, gave Frank the opportunity to go round and meet some of his old pals again.

During the time Frank was filming, Anna Neagle put her foot down regarding his sporting activities. He had signed for Wingate, the London soccer club, which was named after the famous general and was started by ex-Burma servicemen. They wanted Frank to play centre-forward whenever he could and he enjoyed playing with them.

When this was mentioned, Anna would not agree to Frank playing football, not with a film in production. She said he would be no good to them if he broke his ankle whilst playing soccer. Instead, he took up all-in wrestling! He carried this on even after the film was finished, and used to go to a gymnasium in Battersea where some of the Olympic wrestlers taught him different throws.

One Sunday during filming, he was dressed up as a Teddy boy waiting to shoot a scene near Lime Street Station, when he spotted Ronald Shiner getting out of a taxi with all his luggage, ready to go back to London. Frank dashed over, looking, he thought, like a real wide-boy, grabbed Ronald's bags and nipped off into the station with them. Ronald did not have a clue who Frank was. All he knew was that his bags had vanished and he raced after Frank yelling for him to stop. Frank let Ronald catch up with him when he got to the platform for the London train. Ronald could not believe his eyes when he saw it was Frank who had run off with his luggage.

When they were looking for suitable songs for this film, Bert came up trumps once again. He thought the number he had in mind could be just right. He played it over and they all liked it. The song was called "Isn't This a Lovely Evening?" and was introduced into the film.

When the film was screened, Frank was awarded the Picturegoer Medal, and was named most promising new comer. It was the first of a series of films that he would be offered. He made two more films for Herbert Wilcox Productions. These were 'Wonderful Things' from which came the song 'The Heart of a Man' and 'The Lady is a Square'. Actor/singer Anthony Newley appeared in 'The Lady is a Square' playing the part of Frank's brash manager Freddy. Tony was watching Frank making a recording for the film, and the producer commented that Frank was quite good. Newley joked, "Yes, very good, he is another Frankie Vaughan".

Frank was filming the final sequences of "The Lady is a Square" at Talk of the Town, London but filming went on well into the afternoon. He was due to leave on the 4.30 train for Carlisle to begin his Boys' Club tour. His then secretary, Edna Davis, got a telephone call asking her to pack his suitcase for the week and take a taxi to meet Frank so that he could make a dash to the station. She did as requested only to find herself held up by traffic. It was due to a big exhibition in town, which had opened that day.

Edna was sure she would not make it in time and that Frank would miss the train. It was the last train that day and if he did not make it, the whole tour would have to be re-arranged. When Edna eventually got there, she found
Frank and his Manager, sitting in another taxi. They hastily transferred the luggage and off they went with twelve minutes to go. He just managed to make the train in the end.

CHAPTER 19

It was 1959 and life was about to change for Frank and Stella in a big way. Frank was in the USA on another tour of a Vegas nightspot. He was playing the famous Sands and the Dunes. He would then appear in New York playing the Copacabana and The Rainbow Room.

It was while he was playing the Dunes, that Marilyn Monroe came incognito, to see the show. Frank's agent was contacted to discuss the possibility of him appearing in a film with Monroe, which was due to go into production, if it was acceptable to all concerned. There was little doubt that this would make Frank's name known throughout the USA.

He and his agent discussed it in depth, and found all to be in order. It was also to star the French actor Yves Montand. The film was to be called 'Let's Make Love', and would be filmed at Paramount studios in Hollywood. The Director was George Cukor and it would be produced by Jerry Wald. It was arranged that Frank would live in a bungalow in the area where most of the stars lived. The bungalow was luxurious, and included its own swimming pool.

Before long, Frank was missing Stella and the children very much. He wanted them with him as soon as possible. There was the usual film land gossip regarding Monroe and Frank. She made it clear she would like to be more than friends, but there had never been any scandal regarding Frank and the ladies. He made it quite clear that he was married and he would never risk harming his family in any way. They meant the world to him. He never left anyone in doubt that Stella was the only woman for him.

Stella was busy back home, getting everything organised for the journey. There was a lot of work involved in making such a long journey with two children, as David and Susan were still very young.

However, Stella managed to re-unite the family with Frank before too long. The children had missed their father, and they were all so happy to see each other. Frank immediately explained to Stella that there was no truth in the press talk, and gossip.

Stella never doubted that Frank was telling the truth as Monroe had a reputation in Hollywood. He told Stella that Monroe had offered to teach him his lines. Stella replied, "Don't worry Frank, I will read your lines with you", and she did! Frank was never contented with the Hollywood scene. It was not his kind of life at all. He and Stella did not go to lavish parties with the Hollywood set.

He had asked Sammy Cahn to write a song for him. Sammy and Jimmy Van Heusen wrote the whole score for the film including a song called "Incurably Romantic" which Frank later released on a C.D.

By now, all Stella and Frank wanted was to go back home to England, but he was contracted for one more movie. He had no choice but to honour it. The new film, which was called "The Right Approach", starred Gary Crosby, son of Bing. Also Martha Hyer and Juliet Prowse. Frank said it was not his type of film and was out of character for him. The crunch came when he saw that his life was being contracted away and that there was no time for Stella or the children. Then the studio publicity machine started to miss Stella out of things, insisting that Frank appear at first nights with starlets. It just was not the kind of life that Frank or Stella wanted.

Frank had signed a six-year contract but, after making the film he grew so disenchanted with the lifestyle of Hollywood, that he tore up the contract and returned to Britain. The British press made it clear that his fans back home would not like his latest film and it did not get a lot of exposure in England. Stella and Frank were now free to come home.

They could not get back to England quick enough, and to come home to a Palladium season with wonderful artistes and to meet up with friends such as comedian Tommy Cooper, was the icing on the cake for Frank. For a while, when interviewed Frank was always asked about his time in Hollywood. He would only say that when the offer was first made, he thought Hollywood would be wonderful. After a while, he realised that there was nothing wonderful about it. They did not want to know about him being a happy family man and he was strongly advised not to disclose the fact that he was. He realised he could not and would not live a double life. At his initial chat with the director and production team he was grilled quite intensively. He was also told not to spend too much time in the sun as this would darken his complexion.

It was later reported that if he had been prepared to live in the USA, he would have made a fortune, but it was not for him and his family.

Frank did eventually return to America a few years later. During an immensely successful cabaret season at the Rainbow Grill in the Rockefeller Centre, New York, he was approached to play the title role on Broadway in a show based on the life of Harry Richman. He was an American entertainer born in Cincinnati, Ohio in 1885. He was a singer, dancer, comedian, pianist, bandleader, songwriter and nightclub performer. He was born Harold Reichman but changed his name at the age of 18. He died in 1972 aged 77 years. Frank declined the offer to play Richman in the film. He thought the months away from his family and his home was not worth even considering. By now, he wanted to get back home and continue with is normal theatre engagements entertaining his audiences.

CHAPTER 20

He arrived home to great acclaim from his fans. Stella began getting things back to normal at home, whilst Frank's agent set about lining up theatre dates for him to get him back on stage.

He was appearing at the London Palladium in 'Startime' and was more than pleased to be working with his long time friend, Tommy Cooper. Frank knew there would not be a dull moment with Tommy around. Also in the show were singer Cilla Black and Peter Goodright. The show was a huge success, and broke all previous records held at the time. It ran for thirty-four weeks.

The show is long remembered for Tommy Cooper fooling people with a Frankie Vaughan impersonation, which bought the house down. Frank loved it. Tommy always held Frank in very high regard, and considered him to be one of the greatest entertainers in show business in many years.

That year Frank was presented with a special baton by the Musical Director's Association for 'The Most Co-operative Artiste Of The Year', and a Wine Carafe from New Musical Express again when he became 'Top British Favourite Vocal Personality' in a 1959/60 poll.

With the money Frank had earned in America, he and Stella found a plot of land in a green and leafy area of London and had their dream home built. They built a house suitable for a big family. Stella and he designed the kind of home they had always wanted to accommodate their family. When they saw the finished house, they fell in love with it. Frank had his golf club almost next door, and he could very easily reach his fishing spots up the M1 and A1. Stella eventually took up fishing and became pretty good at it, she was almost a match for Frank. It was a very quiet environment and yet not too far to the West End. They were very happy and felt they could settle down completely. They already had David and Susan, Andrew was born after they moved to their new home. It was a comfortable family home with a luxurious lounge, which doubled as a fully equipped recording studio, the electronic gadgetry being concealed behind wooden panelling when not in use.

Over the years, the walls became adorned with many photographs including those taken of Frank with Her Majesty the Queen and other members of the Royal Family taken at such Royal occasions as Command Performances. Photographs of Frank as 'King Rat' of the Grand Order of Water Rats. However, he had a cabinet in the bedroom where he kept his trophies and awards, away from the living area. He thought, "That would be a bit naff". In the cabinet were the cups for fly-fishing, golf and Showbusiness Personality of the Year award. He even had one award for winning the Yorkshire Crooning Competition when living in Leeds years ago.

For their ruby wedding in 1991, Stella bought a two-roomed chalet on the River Thames. It was only a short distance from their home but she and Frank would stay there - sometimes for days on end. It was very restful and away from the telephones. Only one thing seems to have given them real sorrow over the years that was the break-up of the marriages of both David and Susan. It was extremely upsetting for the whole family and it took a long time for everyone to recover from the experience.

Frank's mother Leah naturally thought the world of her son and was very proud of him. As soon as it had become financially possible, Frank had bought his mother a flat of her own in Leeds. He would visit her whenever he could or if he was unable to visit, he would telephone to make sure she was all right. He paid her a visit one time and remarked how cold it was in the hallway of her flat. He told her she must have a radiator installed and to ring his accountant so that it could be arranged for her. She did nothing about it, she felt that over the years, Frank had given her so much and although he was now earning a lot of money, he had given large amounts to needy causes. When he called her after working abroad for a while, the first thing he asked was had she had the radiator fitted.

It seemed that Frank had always been a caring person even when a young boy. At the time, his mother had a small clothing shop in Lancaster, and while she was serving in the shop one day, Frank came in with a young friend from school. He said nothing to his mother but took a bag from the shop and went upstairs. When he came down, there was something in the bag and he handed it to his friend. As she was still serving the customer she and could not ask about it.

Later, when she asked him what it was had been in the bag he had given to his friend, he told her that the boys at school were laughing at his friend because the knees were out of his trousers and the elbows out of his jacket. So Frank had given the boy his own coat and trousers.

Years later, Frank's mother Leah eventually moved to live at the Jewish Home for the Aged in Southport.

CHAPTER 21

August 24 1960 saw the Premiere of the film "Let's Make Love" With Frank and Marilyn Monroe at the Carlton Cinema, Haymarket, London. All proceeds once again went to the Boys' Clubs. Frank was also the subject of "This is Your Life" on American television. He had no idea it was going to take place. He was appearing in Las Vegas when he was asked to go to Los Angeles to do a benefit show. He was flown L.A. and driven to the studio but when he arrived, he was confronted by Ralph Edwards with the Red Book. He was the first British artist to be on "This is Your Life" in America. All his family had made the journey to be there on this special occasion. His parents were flown over from their home in Leeds.

Before this however, he was involved in something much more serious. Frank was asked to play a concert in Glasgow. He was appalled by the levels of violence in this city. One of the more troublesome areas was Easterhouse housing estate. Not only were gangs a problem, but also the problems faced by families living in the very run down houses was a major concern.

Easterhouse was built around 1950 as the run down areas and slums were due to be demolished. It was one of three major housing schemes built as a result. Easterhouse population was around 80,000 at the height of its boom, being split into different areas such as Barlanark, Provanhall and Blairtummock, and others. New homes were built mostly of three storeys high tenements. These had all the modern conveniences of the day, including indoor toilet, two bedrooms, living room and kitchen. This would include two sinks, one of which was deeper for washing clothes, and a wringer and a boiler.

Most of the houses were heated by a coal fire that also heated the water from a back boiler situated behind the fire. We can remember this type of system being built in their hundreds in other parts of the country too. The pipes would then run from the boiler to the kitchen sink. Although there was no central heating in these houses or in most other houses in those days, they were absolute luxury compared to the old dwellings that they had replaced.

There were no recreation facilities, cinemas, shops and places of worship for a few miles. These could only be reached by taking a fifty minute bus journey to the city centre. The same journey would also have to be taken to reach places of work.

Young people, with nothing to do, usually hung around the streets in the evening either kicking a ball around and being a nuisance to other residents or trying to attract the attention of the girls. The girls were much more free to move from area to area, whereas the boys stayed very much within there boundaries which were the main roads of the areas. This lack of facilities and things to occupy themselves soon saw the beginning of the gangs, which at times fought running battles across he roads, mostly throwing stones and pieces of wood torn from garden fencing. It was very unusual for the fighting to cross these borders. In those days drugs were sometimes taken but only by very few.

The running battles during the weekend sometimes became more serious due to alcohol being drunken. These cases began to appear in the local press and the gangland culture of Easterhouse estate was born. Many attempts were made by the police to eliminate this behaviour; schools were opened in the evening where classes were offered along with coaches in the gym where youngsters could take up some sort of sport. Unfortunately, the territorial issues were deeply rooted.

Stories started to appear in the national press of Frankie Vaughan's involvement in working with youngsters in London. The local politicians and police made contact with Frank and he kindly offered to come up to Glasgow and attempt to bring the gangs together. This relationship lasted for many years.

Frank was asked if he could help in any way. Needless to say, he was very pleased to be asked and said he would help in any way he could. He met with the Easterhouse Project Committee, and the City Council to decide the best approach. Easterhouse Project was a scheme to help young people in a notoriously gang-dominated area of Glasgow. He worked closely with Denis Howell, who was the Minister for Sport at that time, to tackle what Frank called "a terrifying situation".

Frank found that one of the main problems was the lack of activities for young people, with no clubs of any kind. He and the Councillors, made an approach to the gang leaders. The names of these gangs were "Drummie", "Pak", "Rebel" and "Toi". To everyone's relief, they all agreed to meet Frank. He had already been involved in helping youths in Liverpool find alternatives to violence through the Boys' Clubs of Great Britain.

It was decided that if the gangs would put down their weapons, Frank would do his best to get a club built with the help of the local Council. The agreement was that the gang would dispose of their weapons at a fixed time and date. Three gang leaders said they would agree to this if the fourth leader agreed. Unfortunately, he was in Glasgow's Barlinnie jail at that time. Frank decided to go to the jail to talk to him. Finally, he agreed to go along with the other gang leaders. Frank was delighted when, at midnight on waste ground beside St. Benedict's Church, many dustbins were filled with all kinds of knives and hammers, which could cause terrible injuries to people. Frank organised the "Not the Gang Show" fundraiser, which sparked the birth of the Easterhouse Project.

True to his word, Frank got in touch with the army to arrange for a very large marquee, as a start. The army did a great job. Lots of equipment was installed including snooker and tennis tables. To raise funds for the club, a concert was arranged with a popular group at that time, The Marmalade. Frank himself appeared too. From 1964 he served on the Home Office Standing Committee on Juvenile Delinquency.

From the outset, he continually called on the Home Secretary, as he was not content to be a passive member. He would ask for more vigorous action to combat a problem of which he had first hand knowledge.

Frank returned to Glasgow in November 1997, this time to open new facilities for disabled and elderly people in Easterhouse, and he is still fondly remembered in the city to this day.

Despite all the hard work and effort made by everyone concerned, a few years later there was a possibility that the Easterhouse Project would close due to lack of funds. However, it was possible that it could continue on a part-time basis. Frank was very upset, as he and others had done all they could to keep the project alive. They were all trying very hard to raise more money to make sure it did not close. Sadly the Easterhouse Project had to close due to the lack of funding.

One thing which really upset Frank was the often-hostile reaction of organisations and people he had to turn down. So many letters arrived at his home asking for donations and personal appearances that, in the end, he had to stop sending individual replies. Instead, he sent out a standard letter saying he would like to help but was so heavily committed that he regretfully could not become involved with any new venture for the time being. This sometimes provoked quite nasty replies. People were writing such terrible things, which upset Frank and his secretary very much.

After reading of attempts to revive Easterhouse, Frank's son David Sye, paid a visit to Easterhouse on the 7 November 2008. He thought it was a great idea to get the project going again and offered his support to the initiative. He is hoping that bringing attention to the situation something can be done. He said he was delighted to lend a hand in Easterhouse, as it was "important that we don't forget what is happening on our own doorstep".

The campaign to get a new Easterhouse Project up and running is being lead by Blairtummock and Rogerfield Tenants and Residents Association (BARTAR). Its Chair, Richard McShane, said the original project had closed due to a lack of funding.

"When Frankie Vaughan came here 40 years ago people were being stabbed and murdered" he said. "He made a real difference and there's no doubt that it saved lives. We want a new community hall built on the site where the Easterhouse Project used to be". "There are a lot of youth projects on the go now but no central meeting place for young people and we feel that a new facility could have a similar impact to the one in the 1960s". David is expected to meet local high school pupils and members of the community after a schedule of events is worked out in advance of his visit.

CHAPTER 22

Frank was appearing in 'Summer Stars' at the Hippodrome, Brighton. Other personalities appearing were Tommy Cooper, Roy Castle, and The King Brothers singing group among others.

Roy Castle was a much loved entertainer who had his big break when he was chosen for the Royal Variety Performance in 1958. He was relatively unknown at that time but made quite an impression on the audience. He was born in Yorkshire and although he was only 28 when he got his big break he had been in show business since the age of 13 years. In that time he had been a comedian, dancer, singer, pianist, guitarist, stooge and talented jazz trumpet player. He was married to Fiona and they had two daughters and two sons.

During the sixties, Roy appeared frequently on television and had his own Roy Castle Show for the BBC. He became an OBE on 31 December 1992. In January that year he had been diagnosed with lung cancer and underwent chemotherapy and radiotherapy and went into remission in the autumn of that year. Roy was a non-smoker and blamed his illness on years of playing the trumpet in smoky jazz clubs. In 1993 he found that the illness had returned and sadly he died in September 1994, he was just 62 years of age.

A charity in his name, Roy Castle Lung Cancer Foundation, was set up and is still the only British charity entirely dedicated to defeating lung cancer. Cliff Richard, who was a friend of Roy, opened the International Centre for Lung Cancer Research in Liverpool. The ceremony was also attended by Sir Harry Secombe, Gloria Honniford and Frankie Vaughan, who was another very good friend of Roy. After the ceremony, the party departed for a celebration lunch and later a fund raising dinner and all-star cabaret.

CHAPTER 23

Each year Frank's schedule seemed equally as busy as the previous one. 1961 was no different. In February, he was again the subject of "This is Your Life" but this time at Trade Hall, Manchester. Holding the Red Book was Eamon Andrews. Frank was also once more on the list of performers at the Royal Command Performance at the Victoria Palace, London.

The BBC used to run a TV programme called Picture Parade. This was a weekly review of the film world which was presented by Peter Haigh and the actor Derek Bond. The programme ran for many years and Peter Haigh regularly interviewed visiting Hollywood stars, including Joan Crawford, Bob Hope, John Wayne, Tyrone Power and Anna Neagle.

It was decided to include a feature on fan clubs in their programme. Jack Bond, the then National Secretary of Frank and Friends, was asked if he would agree to the club being included. Frank was to make an appearance and possibly some of his fans. It was decided that any fans to be invited along, should have their names drawn by lot. Frank suggested they could use his top hat but he thought it would not be quite big enough, Stella thought otherwise!

People sometimes sneer about Fan Clubs but Frank was always very proud of his. Through it, he had made many good friends, and the fans themselves had become friends with one another. He felt that the club had become an association of friends.

After Picture Parade he was away from home for almost four months. First stop was a week at Stockton-on-Tees, and then on to Blackpool. He played at the Palace theatre and once again had a full house. However, he was sad to know that this old theatre was yet another one that was due to be pulled down. The theatre closed in 1961 and was replaced by Lewis's department store. This was eventually replaced by Woolworths and Harry Ramsden's Restaurant.

After Blackpool, he had a short fishing holiday and immediately afterwards he appeared in the annual Boys' Club show at the Royal Festival Hall. The following day he flew to Edinburgh to commence a week of concerts and personal appearances up and down Britain in aid of the Boys' Club movement.

Frank's latest recording "Tower of Strength" had been released and in December it shot to the top of the hit parade. It remained there for four consecutive weeks, and at the end of December, he was awarded a Silver Disc for the recording. It also topped the Hit Parade in Israel for several weeks.

Immediately after Christmas, he had a week of one-night stands, when he would again be working with the King Brothers. Also on the bill was Harry Worth, who was a British comedy actor, now remembered for his 1960s series, 'Here's Harry'. The famous opening credits featured Harry stopping in the street to perform an optical illusion involving a shop window. He would raise one arm and leg whilst standing in the doorway of the shop, the reflection in the window would give the impression of both legs being in the air at the same time. Reproducing this effect was popularly know as "doing a Harry Worth".

The following year, Frank had an unusual engagement to carry out on 21st of January. It was to appear on BBC TV, making the Sunday Night Appeal for the National Association of Boys' Clubs. He was a little worried, as he had not made a television appeal before, and was hoping he could make a good job of it. He had no need to worry, it turned out very well.

CHAPTER 24

When approached about the possibility of having his image created to stand in Madame Tussauds Waxworks in London, Frank was really . When it was completed, he went along to the unveiling of his wax figure. The model was dressed in evening clothes holding a top hat and cane. It was explained to him just what goes into these creations. It takes four to five weeks to make such a model. Three and three quarter ounces of hair were used for Frank's head and each strand had to be inserted into the wax separately. Apparently, this took one girl almost a month to complete and much of the hair comes from convents! He was delighted with the results however, and commented, "So that is what I look like on stage?"

When he began a nine-week engagement at the Talk of the Town, Frank found it quite strange to start work at 11.30 at night. However, these unusual hours did give him more time for himself and the family during the day. He was enjoying the chance to stay at home for a while.

During the first week of October, Frank appeared in a variety show at the Grand Theatre, Wolverhampton. When this was completed, he and Stella decided to take a long overdue ten day summer holiday! Even though they had to take it so late in the year, it gave them time to relax and enjoy the break.

Immediately after their holiday, Frank carried out his usual annual tour of the Boys' Clubs. It ran from 22 October to 27 October. These were spread between London, Cornwall, South Wales, Liverpool and Northamptonshire. When he saw the tour details, he jokingly commented that perhaps someone should donate a helicopter to the Boys' Clubs. He really enjoyed these visits seeing all the young people but they were pretty exhausting.

Next on his agenda was an appearance at the Sunderland Empire for a week during November, where he received great reviews.

Frank must have been one of the most travelled performers in show business as in the spring of 1962 he appeared on a television show and a radio programme in Madrid. The previous week he was in Cyprus entertaining our troops out there and before that, he had a televised show in Copenhagen. On the plane to Copenhagen, Frank had written a song called "I'm Gonna Clip Your Wings" and was hoping that his fans would like it when it was released later in the year.

He had hardly returned from Spain when he was off yet again, this time to Cologne. Negotiations were taking place for him to visit Israel, Scandinavia, and Japan as well as the United States.

His next television show was Sunday Night at the London Palladium in May. At the beginning of July, he was appearing in London's West End for a spell, followed by an autumn nationwide one-night stand tour. He was surprised and of course delighted to hear that, his version of "Tower of Strength" had topped the Hit Parade in Israel for several weeks.

In December that year, he played in his first Christmas pantomime "Puss in Boots" at the London Palladium. It included singer Joan Regan, and comedians Jimmy Edwards, Mike and Bernie Winters and Dick Emery. It ran for fourteen weeks. In the New Year, while having a meal, he unfortunately had a chicken bone stuck in his throat. This caused him to miss a performance for the first time in his career. He seemed to be unlucky with chicken, as it was the second time this had happened to him with a chicken bone.

Although Frank and Stella kept a kosher house, sometimes this was very difficult when eating out or when Frank was travelling and performing. One of Frank's favourite foods was the home made chicken soup which Stella made. He said she made it like no one else could do.

As the children grew a little older, whenever possible, Stella travelled with Frank to his engagements. There was never a question of her not being able to travel with him even when the children were young. One of Frank's or Stella's sisters or one of their mothers would always look after the children.

She would drive Frank to and from his shows. Sometimes she would have to drive through the night in the snow or when it was foggy feeling that the whole world was asleep. Especially when she was driving home at 3am in the morning. For all that, she would not have had it any other way; she preferred to be with him.

CHAPTER 25

A group of musicians was formed to accompany Frank from May 1962 when he had been appearing at the New Theatre, Oxford. These seven men were called the V-Group. These musicians were real fun loving men and enjoyed a joke or two between them and Frank. There was some speculation as to what the 'V' stood for; some of the suggestions they came up with were Volunteers, Vagabonds, Vampires, Villains and Vultures. Actually, it stood for Volunteers. Frank said this was because they never were paid! Jimmy Benson joked about the men who made up the group and wrote the following, tongue in cheek of course.

The V-Group consisted of:

PETER HOUCHIN   **Bass**

Peter is the tallest of the group, he is 6ft 1in tall. He fits this lot, with his bass and amplifier into a Mini Minor, and is mad about ravioli, spaghetti and Italians. He is also a qualified Witch Doctor. Previous bands included Eric Delaney and Frank Weir.

RONNIE LOWLES   **Guitar**

Joined the group on May 21st 1962, at Torquay. Ronnie is the personality boy, he is the one who jumps about the stage, whirling like a Dervish, and generally distracts Frank. He is a great balloon dancer, and is a Lancers and Quadrilles gold medallist. Lives in Brighton and is a spendthrift.
Previous bands included Ronnie Keene, Harry Leader.

ALEX McINNES   **Trombone**

Alec made his debut at Shrewsbury on June 4th and had never looked back-or forward. He is a keen fisherman and still uses his original bait, which Frank gave him well over a year ago. Loves swimming, particularly in trout streams. His striking resemblance to Lord Hailsham had done much to further his career, and he tells me has a very safe seat. Drives a very fast continental car, and sometimes a very slow Pontiac. Is rather accident prone.
Previous bands: Accompanying orchestra to Sammy Davis Senior, Peggy Lee Junior and Betty Hutton.

WILL FYFFE   **Piano**

It has been said of Bungie - as he is affectionately known - that he is the non-playing captain, but I dismiss this as sheer jealousy. I prefer to think of him as a born leader of men, a tower of strength in the rhythm section, and a brilliant linguist, speaking fluent Scottish and English - when he is permitted to speak.

Previous bands: Ronnie Hilton's rhythm ensemble, Dr. Cracks Crockpots, Debroy Summers, The Edgar Allan Poe Chamber Orchestra.

RONNIE HUGHES   **Trumpet**

Ronnie is the best-dressed man in the band. Wears 'casuals' like nobody can. Always to be seen in the best West End clubs, and is an international playboy of some repute. Drives a 1927 Model 'T' Ford. His hobbies are women and 'sitting in' with Aberystwyth Town Silver Prize Band.

Previous bands: Ted Heath and Ivy Benson.

JOHNNY HUGHES   **Saxophone**

No relation to the lovely Ron, but a nice fella in spite of that. John is the noisy one in the band, and is also the band spokesman in case of any disagreements with 'Sir'. Does The Times crossword every day.

Previous bands: Oscar Rabin, Billy Ternent amongst others.

Modesty forbids me to write of the youngest and most handsome member of the group, I will leave that to my lady wife:-

JIMMY BENSON   **Drummer & Philanthropist**

A sensitive, retiring slip of a lad, weighing a mere 17 stones - give or take a pound. Jimmy never speaks unless spoken to, and then only in a whisper. He is s staunch teetotaller, and tries to enlighten his colleagues on the evils of alcohol and tobacco - difficult task for one so young.

Hobbies: adding to his butterfly collection and bird watching. Pet hates: Music and work.

Previous bands: too numerous to mention, discharged with ignominy from them all.

These make up the V-Group, every one a gem, strung together they make a fine string of beads. If you wish to approach them after a show, please bring food and money; then, through an interpreter, they will talk to you. Please be kind to them, because they love all of you.

Goodness knows what kind of high jinks that went on when they were rehearsing, I am sure they had lots of laughs and enjoyed themselves immensely. The V-Group was to accompany Frank for a number of years.

CHAPTER 26

Frank was booked for a concert at Scarborough, and later he had three more to play in Blackpool. Before this however, he was off to Germany for a few days to entertain the British Forces there. From there he headed to Copenhagen where he was booked for a season at Tivoli Gardens. He received a terrific reception as he always found the Danes to be lovely people with a knack of making everyone feel at home. His recording of "Hey Mama" stayed in the Danish hit-parade for 14 weeks and even reached number one. When he returned home, he started work at M.G.M. studios at Borehamwood on his new film, 'It's All Over Now'.

Before he knew it, October was round again, and it was time for Frank to carry out his usual annual tour of the Boys' Clubs. In eight days Frank, along with Will Fyffe and Neville Goodridge, his organising secretary, visited thirty-two Boys' Clubs, four record shops, opened one ladies hairdressing salon, one coffee bar, met fifteen Mayors and other Civic Heads and took part in Big Boy's Club Shows at the Festival Hall, London, and the Palace Theatre, Manchester. Conducted auction Sales, posed for photographs with over five hundred people, took part in Club Competitions and concerts and signed about three thousand autographs! All this was in aid of Boy's Club Funds.

Over one million copies of Frank's records had been sold in aid of the Boys' Clubs. As he was receiving one penny per record this would amount to around £4166 for the clubs, a lot of money at that time. To celebrate the event and to show Frank how much they appreciated his loyalty, friendship and generosity, Lord Althorp, their Chairman at that time, presented him with a Golden Key - the first ever to be presented.

The Club visits started at Ingatestone in Essex with a club for the physically handicapped boys, and then on to Dagenham and Ilford. Next day they travelled by aeroplane to Belfast, where he met the latest Fan Club Branch Secretary. On then to Glasgow where he received a warm reception in the an area of Glasgow called the Gorbals.

This was followed by a visit to Leeds, the West Riding, and a hectic run from Morley to Dewsbury and by Saturday morning, he was in Bradford. The afternoon was spent in Manchester visiting six clubs in a row, followed by a lovely Fan Club Dance organised by Eileen Graham and the Manchester Branch of his Fan Club.

Frank, Will and Neville went on to a supper party with thirty members of the Fan Club. They had a great time but by 2.20 am, they were all ready to retire. Will and Neville went back to spend the night at their hotel and Frank spent the night with cousins. Fortunately, this was the night when the clocks are put back so they did manage to catch up on some sleep.

The concert at the Palace theatre Manchester was a great show. As usual, Frank gave a brilliant performance and the Boys' Club acts were first class. He then headed back down South where he made a quick visit to the Battersea Boys' Club. His final day was to be in Surrey with a tremendous reception in Camberley, Guildford and Wimbledon. By this time, the three men them were almost on their knees, but happy in the knowledge that the Boys' Clubs had had a great boost.

It was past midnight when they arrived at the front door of Frank's home where Stella was waiting to welcome them. They all agreed that it had been the best Club tour they had ever made. These tours took a lot of hard work and organisation so not surprisingly, as this tour ended, they began to start thinking about the tour for next year.

Eventually, the Boys' Clubs started to accept girls and the clubs were re-names Boys' and Girls' Clubs.

CHAPTER 27

In February 1964, Frankie Vaughan was one of 40 people who agreed to serve on the Home Secretary's standing advisory committee on juvenile delinquency. The headmistress of Prince's Park Girls' Secondary School, Liverpool, (Miss L Meyer) was also on the committee. She was secretary of Freeman House Junior Youth Club in Liverpool.

Among the other advisors were Mr Henry Brooke, a barrister for Queens Council in 1981 and Knighted in 1988 when he became Sir Henry Brooke. He was to be chairman of the committee. Mountaineer Sir John Hunt, a Nottingham magistrate from the West Indies, and a Jamaican girl working in Birmingham. The committee met for the first time at the Home Office.

Members were selected not as representatives of particular interests, but for their personal qualities. Each had first-hand knowledge of young people and their problems in some capacity. Frank for instance, was described by the Home Office as "an entertainer with active interest in youth work".

Near the end of the year, the committee members were unhappy at the absence of any information notified to the public of the ground the committee had covered and the ideas examined. In the months since it was set up, a number of suggestions had been made, some by experts, on the subject of juvenile delinquency. These were thought to be informative to various agencies and people concerned with juvenile wrongdoing, by no means least, parents. The committee felt that an interim report or memorandum would stimulate interest in the work of the committee.

Later that year, Frank took his Keystone Cops cricket team to Blenheim Palace for the annual match against Oxford University. His team included Paul Cave, Frank's manager at that time, as wicket keeper, Bernard Bresslaw as clown, Roy Castle, actor Sidney Tafler, Tony Craxton of the BBC, Peter Goodright who was appearing in Frank's show at the Palladium, and a few county players. It attracted a crowd of over 10,000. The team had played at Lord's the day before and the crowd had been around 4,000.

The University went in first and, with the help of the clowning in the field where the Keystone Cops quarrelled about who should run for the ball, made a decent score of 238. Mike Groves from South Africa scored 67 including 24 from one over when Frank put himself in to bowl. Frank managed to get his own back when his next over had Groves stumped by Paul Cave. Mike Groves was a professional cricketer born in January 1943. He had played for Oxford University, and Somerset. Everyone had a great time at Blenheim and the proceeds amounted to over £1,000 for the local Boys' Clubs.

The same year also saw the release of Frank's hit song "Hello Dolly" which was written for the American musical of the same name. His recording was released much later than originally planned. A fire at the offices of the music publishers, Chappels, caused a number of late releases. Obviously, it caused a great many problems and subsequently records, including Frank's, were late being released. When if finally was released, it received a great reception by the public, and was in the charts for quite some time.

CHAPTER 28

In February 1965, Frank accepted the invitation from the National Boys' Club to become its president. He already set aside one week each year for the sole purpose of visiting the clubs round Britain. He was awarded the OBE in the 1965 Birthday Honours for 'services to the welfare of youth'. It was a very proud moment for Frank and his family when the award was presented by Her Majesty the Queen. His mother was there to see him receive the award and knew how proud Frank's grandmother would have been to see him received such an honour.

Frank was offered his very first television series which meant spending many hours each day in the television studios recording each episode. It was shown every Saturday evening for six weeks from 21 August. This meant that he was almost living at the A.T.V. studios at Borehamwood, but he really enjoyed doing it. He was joined by some old friends, such as Bruce Forsyth, comedian Arthur Haynes, Jimmy Tarbuck, comedy actresses Hattie Jacques and Dora Bryan.

In May that year, Frank and Jimmy Tarbuck were appearing in a weeklong show at the Coventry Theatre. During a short break from performing, they decided to take a trip to Wembley to see the Cup Final. Liverpool was playing so it was of interest to them both. They decided that they would make the return journey by helicopter. When they saw how small the helicopter was, Jimmy totally lost his nerve and would not travel in it. They then decided to travel home by taxi instead.

Things were about to get more complicated when the taxi broke down on the M1. They started to thumb a lift, but no one stopped for them. Jimmy cannot be serious for long and he jokingly told Frank to kick out his leg, in the hope that maybe someone would take pity on them and give them a lift home.

Eventually, a car did stop for them. The driver was a soldier, and his very pregnant wife. She got very excited when she realised who their passengers were. Jimmy jokingly kept asking Frank to sing a song for the young woman but Frank did not oblige. When they finally arrived back at Coventry, Frank chased Jimmy down the road saying "I'll give you sing her a song".

Jimmy was always known for playing jokes on fellow performers, and Frank was the perfect target. At the end of one show, Jimmy arranged with an old friend of his who was in his sixties, to pretend to be waiting to see Frank at the stage door. Jimmy waited for Frank to finish the show. As he was leaving the theatre, Jimmy started to try to move on the elder gent. It looked terrible to Frank who got very upset, and began to tell Jimmy off. "You shouldn't treat people like that," Frank told him. Jimmy started to laugh, so did the old gent. Frank then realised he had been had, and they all had a good laugh.

Jimmy also told a funny tale of Frank and golf. Jimmy was on the green with a few friends, these included Bernie Winters. Bernie was in a position to take a shot at the ball when Frank strolled by. He looked at Bernie and said "Bernie, if you don't mind my saying so, you are holding the club all wrong. Your right shoulder is too far forward, if you turn slightly the other way you will find it more comfortable". "I just noticed as I was walking by" Bernie said "Well thank you Frank" and Frank carried on with his stroll. Bernie looked at the other players and said, "You want to tell him to p..s off but he is such a lovely man".

Bernie Winters was part of a stand-up comedy double act in the 1960s with his brother Mike. Bernie died in 1991 aged 58.

CHAPTER 29

During August the following year, Frank did three Sunday concerts. These were at Westcliff-on-Sea at the Winter Garden, where he performed only one show. However, at Bournemouth he did one show on 15 August and the other on 29 August. In between these two concerts, he flew to Cannes, France to do a special cabaret there.

The usual Boys' Clubs tour soon came round again and Frank was to carry this out in the last two weeks of that month. This was started with the annual "Clubs Are Trumps" show at the Royal Festival Hall. These shows were launched by Frankie Vaughan in 1956 as a national search for young talent. From Festival Hall, the show moved on to where visits were made to the West Country and the South of England Boys' Club events. Frank also looked forward to the Boy's Club concert at the Palace theatre, Manchester on 24 October.

Towards the end of the year, he started a season at "The Talk of the Town" and, what was a real treat for all the family, they were delighted to be able to spend Christmas and the New Year together, which was quite a rare occasion for them all.

In the spring of 1966, Frank undertook a journey which he had been promising to undertake on a number of occasions. Each time some other commitment prevented him from keeping his promise. He was determined to make it this time. It was the longest journey he would possibly take in his career. It was to carry out a tour of Australia, New Zealand and Hong Kong.

Frank was playing the London Palladium pantomime season in the early sixties when Bob Bryan was selected to be Frankie's back-stage assistant. His job was to see that Frank was spared the every-day happenings or annoyances, arrange his costume changes, meet people on his behalf and act as 'aide de camp' in general.

When performing pantomime, with changes of costume, and when time allowed, having something to eat, the artiste has little time between shows. Meeting the back stage visitors can be time consuming too. Other personalities in show business often visit other artistes appearing at the Palladium. People such as Noel Coward were in the audience and he requested to meet Frank. He always tried to accommodate these people but unfortunately, some of his after show fans had to forego a visit to his dressing room. This was not what he liked to happen as he had a great relationship with his fans. They knew that he never turned them down without good reason.

Such people as Bessie Braddock, Harry Secombe, Tommy Cooper and Charlie Drake and many other big names had at some time called on Frank to congratulate him on his performance. Frank was very fond of Bessie and they became good friends. Elizabeth Margaret Braddock JP, was born Elizabeth Bamber in Liverpool on the 24 September 1899 and later became a Labour politician. She was affectionately known as Bessie. Her mother was Mary Bamber, also an active woman in Liverpool politics. Bessie joined the Labour Party and in 1922 married John 'Jack' Braddock.

Bessie became a councillor in 1930 and in 1945 she became president of the Liverpool Trades Council and Labour Party. She was a member of the Union of Shop, Distributive and Allied Workers for many years. During World War II she worked as an ambulance assistant officer. She was elected Member of Parliament for Liverpool Exchange at the 1945 election and served for 24 years. Bessie was known as an ardent socialist and fiery campaigner, nicknamed 'Battling Bessie'. She was granted the Freedom of the City of Liverpool in 1970, shortly before her death.

Frank was later appearing at Birmingham Hippodrome in pantomime when a couple of months into the run of the show, started to get problems with his hearing. When it was checked, it turned out to be a very painful mastoid which had to be removed at the local hospital. The operation went very well and was very successful.

When he left hospital, of course the local newspaper was quick to report it. A photograph on the front page showed Frank on the steps with a young nurse standing on each side of him. He was so grateful for all the kindness shown to him while he was there; he arranged to pay for a new bed to be donated to the hospital.

In the spring the following year, Frank was asked to open the Tulip Festival, which is held every year in Birmingham's Cannon Hill Park. The organisers decided to fly Frank in by helicopter to the park, which seemed like a good idea. A problem arose when the noise from the helicopter blades affected his ears, due to the recent mastoid operation. When he got out of the helicopter, he could hardly hear a thing as the noise from the helicopter had affected his hearing. Hundreds of people had turned out to see him, and everyone made a big fuss of him. Each year the flower displays were wonderful, and that year was no exception. Happily, Frank's hearing had gradually returned, and he was able to enjoy the show.

Each year was busy for Frank and he always had plenty of engagements to fulfill. From Birmingham, he continued his cabaret work all over England. Then there were the summer seasons, and his charity work for his favourite charity, the Boy's Clubs. He also donated the proceeds of his first record released each year to this charity.

Frank was well known for interest in various sports, fishing being his favourite, but coming very close was golf and football. This lead the Football Association agreeing to his request that he be allowed to lead the 100,000 crowd in the singing of 'Abide with Me' and 'You'll Never Walk Alone' at the 1973 Cup Final. He used this song regularly in his act.

As Frank's first passion was fishing, he had become a very good fisherman. He would go off for the day whenever time permitted. Stella could easily have become a fishing widow but wisely, she decided to try it herself and had her own set of rods. Before long, she became almost as keen as Frank and was pretty good at it too, but she was always careful not to catch the first fish of the day before Frank! Sometimes passers by recognised Frank in his angling habit and did a 'double take.' However, once they realised he was a serious fisherman they would leave him alone.

When David was a young lad he also became interested in fishing, and as he got older, there was quite a lot of friendly rivalry between him and his father. They used to have a contest between them that the first to catch a 5lb trout would be the winner. Frank could not believe it when David landed the first big one. David had it stuffed and mounted in a case and sent the bill to his father! It is still on the wall in his mother's kitchen to this day. Frank however did later win a large trophy for his fishing.

CHAPTER 30

Every year, Frank would take a month off from touring to carry out his annual visits to the boys' clubs; this would usually be in October. He always enjoyed his time with these young lads and loved the interaction with them. At one of the clubs, he decided to put on some boxing gloves, and to spar with one of the youngsters. Some of these lads were pretty good boxers, and Frank ended up with a black eye for his trouble. It was even on the television news but he took it well, and probably had a good laugh about it after.

He made a point of visiting boys' clubs in as many different parts of the country as he could possibly manage in the time allowed. It has been known, for him to get into the wrong car in a dash to visit as many in one day as possible. It happened in the north of England, when he jumped into a car thinking it was his transport to the next boys' club, when it was a complete stranger driving by. The driver was a good sport and saw the funny side of the mistake. He was good enough to take Frank to the next club where he was expected.

I remember one bonfire night somewhere in the late 1960s, Frank was lighting the bonfire at a boys' club in Erdington, a suburb of Birmingham. My wife and I had just moved to a new house with our four young children, not far away from the club. I was in the middle of doing some work on my new home at the time, but we had told the children we would take them to the bonfire. Needless to say, there was a large crowd already there when we arrived. It was difficult to find Frank as he was completely surrounded by children and parents. Because of the crowd, Frank was most concerned about the children's safety but thankfully, it all went off without a hitch, and a good time was had by all.

For the previous few weeks, Frank had been recording an ITV Christmas show with Bruce Forsyth and comedian Frankie Howard. He was about to start an eight-week run in his own "Frankie Vaughan Show" at the Alhambra Theatre in Glasgow. He and Stella had rented a spacious flat in the city over the Christmas holidays for themselves and their three children, David aged 14, Susan aged 11, and Andrew who was two and a half. In the New Year, they would all be back in their own home in North London while Frank would appear in a show in Dunstable for a fortnight. After that, he was hoping to take a rest. He had not taken a holiday for over a year, or a day off - including Sundays - from the beginning of the previous July. Whatever time he takes off professionally, Frank always had time for his charity work.

As well as his devotion to the Boys' Clubs, Frank also had his passion for fly-fishing. It was Eamonn Andrews, another keen fisherman, who taught him to fly fish. He loved to get out on the rivers in the fresh air after the very smoky atmosphere of the clubs. Eamonn was a Dublin born television and radio personality who started his broadcasting career in 1939. Readers may remember him as a presenter of a chat show and children's programmes, but he was best known for the hugely popular and long-running "This Is Your Life" which he ran from 1955-1987. He would surprise celebrities by presenting them with a review of their careers.

He had begun broadcasting with Radio Eireann, and subsequently appeared on various radio shows for the British Broadcasting Corporation (BBC), including Sports Report. As a youngster, he joined a boxing club, and he had a life-long love of the sport. His first television role was as host of the parlour game What's My Line? A member of the public would mime a small part of their profession and the celebrity panel would have to guess their occupation. Eamonn died 1987 at the age of 65 years.

Frank's love of fishing landed him in a bit of trouble. He appeared on a television show in Birmingham called Pebble Mill. Frank went out in a small boat whilst he was wearing his waders. Viewers telephoned the BBC to point out the danger of wearing waders whilst on water in these small boats. Obviously, if he had fallen into the water he could have drowned. He made a full apology, and agreed that it was a bad example to set.

CHAPTER 31

After an exhausting series of engagements that covered all the main cities of Scotland, Frank took Stella away for the weekend to the Lake District. Frank knew the area well having been evacuated there during the war. They decided to stay at the Sharrow Bay hotel on Lake Ullswater, which had been recommended to him. Unfortunately, when they arrived the hotel had been booked several months in advance. However, the couple who owned the hotel insisted that he and Stella stay with them at their house nearby. They were given a magnificent room which was superbly decorated it was just like stepping backing into another world. When Stella and Frank went down to dinner that evening, on the table was a vase of lovely miniature red roses.

Stella and Frank spent their days walking along the beautiful lakeside, pony-trekking. The evenings were spent on the lake and in the lounge listening to music. They loved having time to just talk to each other, something they had very little time to do when Frank was working. Unfortunately, the weekend soon came to an end and it was back to work.

When he returned to work, an incident took place, which upset Frank very much. He had been performing at the London Royal Festival Hall for the RAF Benevolent Fund. After the show and at some point during the evening, his one hundred year old, silver-topped cane went missing back stage. A search was made of the venue but the cane was nowhere to be found. Frank offered £100 reward for the return of his precious cane, which is covered with Chinese figures, and had been part of his act for a long time. He did have a substitute cane but it never felt the same. He was convinced that he would drop the replacement cane when he tried to twirl it during a performance. Fortunately, his much-loved cane was later found in the street near the theatre, and returned to him. It was never discovered how it had gone missing or who was responsible.

Frank was always in great demand for stage work. He made an appearance on Sunday Night at The London Palladium, and was the only performing star to appear on two Sundays consecutively. Although of course, Bruce Forsyth became the long-standing compere at the Palladium. Frank also had his own television show, and had guest stars such as Tom Jones and Engelbert Humperdinck.

Frank was taken by surprise by Eamon Andrews when he approached him with his big red book for "This Is Your Life". He was even more surprised when five young men entered the stage. They had been the gang leaders from Glasgow's Easterhouse. One former gang leader wanted to say how grateful he was for the help that Frank had given to all the young people of Easterhouse. The help they had received had enabled him to sort out his life. He said "Nobody else came, Frankie was the only one. We did not know what we were looking for. Frankie was one of the lads. He brought plans and had a youth club put up". Needless to say, Frank was very touched to hear this, it meant a great deal to him.

CHAPTER 32

The country was devastated when a terrible disaster struck Aberfan, a mining village in Merthyr Tydfil, Wales. October 1966 there had been a deluge of rain for days; this caused a large slagheap to collapse. It completely engulfed a village, and a school full of young children was destroyed. Many people, including the children perished. Everyone throughout the whole country felt the effect of such a disaster.

Later, a charity show was arranged for the people of Aberfan at a London Theatre. Frank was one of the celebrities who gave their time to this show, and an enormous amount of money was raised. Eventually, millions of pounds were raised for this most worthy cause.

Frank was voted "Prince Rat" for 1967 at the annual dinner in London of the Grand Order of Water Rats. This is the Order's second highest honour with only the office of "King Rat" taking precedence over it.

At the dinner Frank was wearing dark glasses. He explained that he had managed to get a black eye at a snooker match between the Water Rats and the Eccentric Club. Some of his team mates of the Rats were so annoyed about him winning his game that they tried to lift him shoulder high - and dropped him head first resulting in the black eye.

During 1967, a number of show business personnel had set up an organisation to provide entertainment for Israeli troops following the hostilities when Israel attacked Egypt. The Organisation for Israel was formed in close liaison with the Israeli Embassy in London. Among the volunteer stars set for tours were units headed by Frankie Vaughan, and fellow singers Tom Jones, Adam Faith, Dusty Springfield, Paul and Barry Ryan and the Searchers. Offers to join the scheme came from the Continent and from America, including Sammy Davies Junior. Paul and Barry were the twin sons of popular British singer of the fifties, Marion Ryan.

They were all warned that it was not going to be a joyride, and if the full benefits were to be realised by the tour, they must take the shows to the outlying areas as far apart as the Sinai Desert and the Upper Galillean and Judean Hills. The artistes taking part were all donating their services.

October that same year, Frank made a fleeting visit to his home town of Liverpool and unbelievably managed to get lost. The City had changed so much since his previous visit that when he tried to find the entrance to the Mersey Tunnel it was not where he thought it was. He was on his way from Stalybridge to Wallasey, where he had attended a party to raise funds for club headquarters at Seacombe. He had eventually found the entrance to the Mersey Tunnel.

There are not many people who would turn down an invitation to attend a reception with the Prime Minister at Number 10 Downing Street, but Frank did! Not because he and Stella did not want to attend but he was otherwise engaged. He was booked to appear at clubs in Barnsley and Batley. The bookings had been arranged a month previous and he did not want to let the people down.

He sent a telegram to explain with his apologies to Mr Wilson, the prime mister at the time. He said that he hoped he and Stella would be invited again when he was in a position to go.

CHAPTER 33

Frank had a full week's engagement at Batley Variety nightclub in Yorkshire, which was the largest club in Great Britain. It was eventually sold and is now called the Frontier. He also attended a show in Birmingham to celebrate his thirty years in show business. It was held at The Night Out, which was the top nightspot in Birmingham at that time. Whenever possible, Stella would travel with Frank to be with him in the wings when he was performing. Over the years she became very competent in setting the lighting and sound systems. When he was ready, Frank would hold up his thumb as if to say "is everything ok?". Stella would sign the same back to say "yes".

The Grand Order of Water Rats was holding a charity show at Kings Cabaret club, Birmingham and Frank was to be Master of Ceremonies for that night. He introduced a new young comedian by the name of Jim Davidson. Also new at that time, was singer Joe Longthorne. They both gave their time free, and later became successful show business personalities.

In affiliation to the boys club of Wales, was the Penygraig club in the Old Wesleyan Chapel on Brook Street, Williamstown. This was opened by Frank in 1974, and has enjoyed much success. It has trained ten football coaches to reach association football standard of Wales.

Frank was appearing at the Night Out club, Birmingham again when the dreadful pub bombings took place. It was November 21 1974, and they were thought to be carried out by the Irish Republican Army (IRA). 21 people were killed and 182 injured. The explosive devices were placed in two pubs in the centre of Birmingham, they were the Mulberry Bush, which was situated at the foot of the tall office block called the Rotunda, and the Tavern in the Town, a pub set in a basement on New Street. This was later renamed the Yard of Ale. A memorial plaque, commemorating the victims of the bombings, is situated in the grounds of St Philip's Cathedral, in the centre of Birmingham.

The following year, a charity Gala was held to raise funds for the victims of the bombings. This was held at the Birmingham Hippodrome and amongst those appearing was television personality Noele Gordon. Frank was top of the bill and Don MacLain, a Birmingham comedian, compared the Gala which was attended by Harold Wilson, the Labour Prime Minister at the time, and his wife Mary. It raised a substantial amount of money for the victims of the bombings.

Frank returned to Birmingham to appear in cabaret at the New Cresta club, Solihull. While in Birmingham, he sang at BBC Pebble Mill, in a Good Old Days Variety Show. On the bill were Norman Vaughan and actor Leonard Sachs, the stars of the show, which was playing at the Birmingham Hippodrome at the time. The programme marked the last appearance of The Good Old Days on BBC television.

While in the Midlands, Frank was asked to be a member of the committee to help tackle drugs. He was very pleased to accept as he hardly ever declined to help with any organisation or charity, no matter the subject.

Frank was appearing in a show in Blackpool when Stella telephoned to give him some lovely news. Their daughter, Susan, had given birth to a baby girl, who they were naming Lillie. Frank was obviously overjoyed at the news, and announced it on stage during the show. Everyone was thrilled for him and Stella. After the show, he drove overnight in order the see his new granddaughter. Susan went on to give birth to two more children during the next few years. They were Jamie and Annabelle.

A few years previously, Susan was studying at the Italia Conti stage school in London to become an actress. She was also a very talented singer with quite a powerful voice. She was considering a career in show business and Frank thought there may be a spot for her in some of his shows.

CHAPTER 34

Like most parents, Frank and Stella only wanted the best for their children. One day, their son, Andrew, told them that he wanted to try America to get the feel of the place. Although he was only twenty years old at the time, his father said he had no objection but warned him about the cost. Frank and Stella had never believed in just handing money to their children. They were always encouraged to get a good education, and to work for what they wanted in life. In fact, Andrew did make a very big effort to get his own money by taking two jobs. He worked for the tax office during the day, and from six to nine in the evening, he sold advertising space on the telephone.

As it turned out, Andrew worked very hard to become an actor. He appeared in a dramatic role playing a James Dean type character. The play was called "Come Back to the Five and Dime Jimmy Dean" at the London East Dulwich Tavern.

Having finished his run in a production by The Partisan Theatre, London, Andrew made his way to the Edinburgh Festival. In a new play called "Into the Clear Space", he played a slimy television producer. Stella and Frank were very proud of him. As Frank always said "It does not matter who your parents are it is the public who make you".

Andrew eventually went to the United States, and has made a fine career for himself. However, he had begun his career on the London stage in such productions as "The Ecstasy", "Bent" and "A Midsummer Nights' Dream", at the Globe Theatre. He also stared in winning productions of musicals such as "Sweet Charity" and "Godspell" coming from Edinburgh festival.

After appearing for two seasons on the UK sitcom "Second Thoughts" as well as a number of commercial appearances, he made his move to the United States. He very soon landed a role in "Nash Bridges" and the film success, "Boyfriends" in 1996. He returned to the UK for his role as Owen, the film's bad-boy.

Back in the US and had a number of television and film credits since then. He has been the voice of the evil "Valmont" in the "Jackie Chan Adventures" and had a role in "Polar Express" with Tom Hanks and Robert Zemekis. He continues to live and work in Los Angeles, California.

David Sye, Stella and Frank's eldest son, became a successful and world famous yoga master. He has been practicing yoga for over 24 years and in 1990 he moved to Yugoslavia to work as a Radio journalist on a non-political radio station, whilst also teaching yoga to classes in Belgrade. Due to unforeseen circumstances he found himself caught up in the middle of the Bosnian war. He returned to the UK in 1995 to continue teaching Yogabeats, which is a distinct Yoga style. He developed this technique while teaching yoga to soldiers during the Bosnian war, using James Brown songs to drown out the bombing.

Over the years David has taught Yogabeats to the Israeli Yoga Teachers Association, the Zurich Birkhram Association, and teacher associations in Italy, Zurich Yoga Teachers Association and Yoga Mosaic (Jewish Yoga Teachers Association). Through Yogabeats pioneering work it is now taught to Palestinians in Jericho and the Territories and after visiting Rammalah the first class is due to take place there very soon.

Teaching yoga in Brixton and the West Bank he said "People disarm before they come to my classes and at the end they are hugging each other. That's just through humanity".

CHAPTER 35

In 1968, the Grand Order of Water Rats chose Frank to hold the position of "King Rat" which is a great honour. He was chosen for the position due to the enormous amount of charity work he had carried out, and the vast sums of money he had raised for various worthy causes. This work must be kept private, which was no problem for "King Rats" as their achievements were never publicised.

At the end of their rein for the year there is a Grand Ball held and the 'King' speaks to the guests. Frank's speech started as follows: "My dear guest of the Grand Order of Water Rats. I have been singing (and kicking!) my way through show business for a few years now but it is true to say that the most kicks in my career have been during my year as King Rat. A lot of thanks are due to a lot of people for that, but firstly let me tell you about some of those kicks".

He then went on to tell of some of the fund raising he was involved with. One of these was the 'Clubs are Trumps' week held each year for fundraising events. The week long events was launched by The Duchess of Gloucester at the Royal Festival Hall, London. After twelve years this was to be the end of this Boys' Club show but everyone concerned were determined to see that it went out with a bang.

As well as fund raising, boys from all over the country, from Scotland to Birmingham, were taking part in the actual show and boys had been auditioning during the year. Frank would be top of the bill supported by Roy Castle and the Band of the Irish Guards.

For one starting event to Club Week in Bridgnorth David Duncan travelled the 135 miles to London on a bed. Nine club members all between the ages of 14 and 16 pushed the bed. David carried messages from the Mayor of Bridgnorth and the Chairman of the Bridgnorth Rural District Council. They were escorted by four adults in the club van. The party, including the bed, left Bridgnorth to travel via Bromsgrove, Stratford-upon-Avon, Banbury, Bicester, Aston Clinton and Bushey before making the last lap into London. This journey took from Monday to the following Sunday.

Clubs along the route were very helpful providing hospitality for the party, who took all their own catering and bedding equipment with them. On the way they made a collection for a Church of England Children's Society. The bed, which was specially donated by the Vono bed company and was to be given to a London Children's home. Such events as these took place all over the country and raised a lot of money for various charities.

Also at the end of this very eventful year, Frank was pleased to hand over to Companion Water Rat the Duke of Edinburgh a very handsome cheque for £4,500 for his Award Scheme - the proceeds of a Greyhound Meeting.

In January he was joined by the entire company of his show at Glasgow Alhambra Theatre on behalf of the GOWR for the city's Disaster Fund. He handed a cheque to the Lord Provost to the value of £1,412 17s 11d for the victims and dependents of those who suffered.

Among the artistes involved with this special show were two wonderful entertainers who gave Frank one of the biggest kicks of his year. They were Steve and Jimmy Clarke, known as the Clarke Brothers, the wonderful tap dancing duo. Steve and Jimmy were born and brought up during the depression in the southern states of America. They started working when they were four years old. Over the years, they shared the bill with Gypsy Rose Lee, Elvis, the Beatles and many other stars. Sammy Davis Junior was their cousin and they taught the British pop groups of the sixties how to dance. They have lived in Britain for many years, and Frank was thrilled to initiate them as Brothers of the Grand Order of Water Rats.

He spoke of his thanks to various artistes who gave their time during the week at Glasgow Alhambra on behalf of his Easterhouse Project. They included fellow Water Rats Jimmy Logan, Jimmy Tarbuck and Derek Roy.

He then expressed his thanks to his wife Stella for her patience and encouragement. He said that all through the year she had been able to witness the great service that the Water Rats had been able to provide not just for their own causes but for so many worthy efforts.

He closed by thanking his fellow Water Rats for such magnificent support, kind-ness and interest during his year in office. He would be handing over the banner of King Rat to another member of the GOWR Harry Seltzer for the year of 1969.

Near the end of Frank's year of office, the world of show business suffered a great loss on 20 October with the death of Bud Flanagan, O.B.E. Bud was born in October 1896 to Polish Jews Wolf and Yetta Weintrop, and began working with Chesney Allen in 1926. They were known as Flanagan and Allen a comedy and singing double act. Bud had been King Rat on three occasions.

Some of the world's most famous people are honorary members of the Grand Order of Water Rats, such as, Laurel and Hardy and Bob Hope. The chorus of The Water Rats Anthem is:

And this is the emblem of our Society
Each member acts with the greatest propriety
Jolly Old Sports, to them we raise our hats
A jolly lot of fellows are the Water Rats

The Water Rats were founded in 1889 a group of music hall stars, the principal star being Joe Elvin, owned a trotting pony called 'Magpie'. The pony was winning a good number of races round London. The winnings were used to help performers who were in trouble or distressed in any way. These performers were among the first to start soup kitchens to feed the poor and the refugees arriving from Eastern Europe.

One day in a torrential downpour of rain, taking the horse back to its stabling, the drive of a horse-drawn London bus spotted the two well-known music hall stars with the sodden pony and yelled, "Blimey, what you got there?" They replied, "It's our trotter". "Trotter, looks more like a blooming water rat".

This inspired the band of performers to re-christen the horse. Their thoughts were that water rats were lowly creatures. They would elevate the lowest to the highest and make it respected in "the firmament of good fellowship and charity". It was also pointed out that "Rats" backwards spells "Star". That summer they all gathered in a pub in Sunbury-on-Thames and formed "The Pals of the Water Rat". The pub was named The Magpie to honour the little pony who started it all. The members of the order continue to raise money for entertainers in need, and medical equipment for hospitals.

Over the past 100 years, the 'Club' progressed to become the 'Grand Order of Water Rats', but the membership has never been more than 200. It is a highly prized honour for a performer to belong to the 'Rats' and it includes some of the biggest stars both in Britain and Hollywood. It also spreads as far as Australia, Africa and Spain.

On Lodge Night, King Rat sits in his chair, which is reminiscent of a throne. He is surrounded by past King Rats. The Prince Rat sits next to the King and the Musical Rat will play something on the piano which is appropriate to the King Rat. This could be All the Nice Girls Love a Sailor if that person has been working on the ships or instance. Frank always got Give Me the Moonlight when he walked in. Newly elected members are called Baby Rats and wear a white collar in Lodge until another initiate takes his place, he then is allowed to wear the red collar of a fully fledged Water Rat, age is irrelevant. If it is found that someone is in any way out of order, King Rat says "Fine that Rat three coins". A Scribe Rat is the person who produces a newsletter, and every member around the world gets a copy of the newsletter.

A smaller group of distinguished gentlemen, who carry out charitable works but are not theatre or television performers, are enrolled as 'Companion Rats'. These include HRH Prince Phillip, HRH Prince of Wales and HRH Prince Michael of Kent. It is an all male society although there is a sister Order in the form of Lady Ratlings, made up of Rat's partners and ladies from the entertainment world.

Regardless of office or position, every Rat has the right to display the gold emblem of the Order in his lapel, which is worn with enormous pride. Every year a new King Rat is elected who is obliged to act as figurehead of the Order. Each successive year King is determined to leave his own mark, not only in governing the Lodge, but in trying to raise record amounts of money for charity. This is done in the form of the many functions and shows, which are organised, the proceeds of which invariably is given to those who most need it.

Novelty boxing matches, Royal Galas, visits, personal appearances, tributes, variety nights and events of all kinds are staged to buy, amongst other things, lifts for ambulances, chair mobiles, intensive care units and medical equipment of every description. Assistance is also given to entertainers who may have fallen upon hard times, and the families of those who have passed on, as well as much involvement with Brinsworth House, the retirement home for elderly performers.

CHAPTER 36

Brinsworth House came about after many meetings and much fund raising by a number of old performers. At the turn of the century, The Music Hall Artistes' Railway Association (MHARA) offered reduced fares and other benefits to its members. This was to enable them to travel to and from engagements. At a meeting of the subscribers to the Association on December 4th 1907, Joe O'Gorman (a King Rat) proposed a levy on the Annual Subscription of one shilling (.05p). The purpose of the levy was to start a benevolent fund for the benefit of its members and fellow artistes.

It was proposed to add additional funds from other sources including voluntary contributions, odd charity matches, the proceeds of the Annual Dinner, collections on liners to and from America, South Africa, and Australia by artistes travelling to and from engagements in those counties. This would provide relief to performers from hardship, and could be available in many ways, including weekly pensions, grants of money, loans to artistes for fares to engagements, fees, funeral expenses and finally for admittance to a Home for performers who through old age were unable to continue to earn their livelihood.

This came about when an idea for a home for old performers of both sexes, was suggested by Joe Elvin in 1908. This was publicised in the professional papers of the day, and at the Annual Dinner of the MHARA, the idea was received with great acclaim, and a large sum of money was immediately subscribed.

At a General Meeting of artistes held at the Old Empire, Camberwell, the details of the project were disclosed and additional monies subscribed until nearly £2,000 was raised. Architect's plans were acquired for the proposed building, and the estimated costs for the building were to be £7,000, a huge amount of money in 1908. Joe Elvin (a King Rat) promised to donate £500 for the purchase of the land.

After a good deal of searching, a mansion near Twickenham, which had been empty for a few years, was found. It was ideal for their requirements, and in August 1911, the property was purchased for £2,400. One thousand was paid in cash from the reserves, and the rest remaining on mortgage.

A Committee comprising of several Water Rats commenced preparing the house for occupation. Obviously, alterations would have to be made; this included a new drainage system as well as some interior decoration. All the work was carried out at a cost of £500. Furnishing was estimated at £280, which was raised by a special Sixpenny Fund organised by "The Performer" newspaper. All work was finally finished two months later, and the house was ready by early November. By the end of November, ten inmates including one married couple took up residence.

In 1913, The Benevolent Fund took over the existing Music Hall home at Gypsy Hill where 10 or 12 old performers were residents. All these moved to Brinsworth House so that all old performers were together.

In 1914, a complete new wing was built and completed in October that year. It was hoped that a member of the Royal Family would perform the official opening, but war broke out and that event had to be postponed. Two new wings have been added over the years and on both occasions the ceremonies were performed by one of its most ardent Patrons HM Queen Elizabeth, The Queen Mother. It still has the support of the Royal Family today. HM The Queen is Patron of the Entertainment Artistes Benevolent Fund (EABF) and the Royal Variety Performance provides a substantial amount of funding to this fund. It is also supported by many other theatrical charities and organisations which includes the Grand Order of Lady Ratlings.

Caring for the residents of Brinsworth House is only part of the work of The Fund. It also devotes its resources to relieving over 300 distressed performers (from all branches of the industry) with aid and financial assistance each week. Many requests for help are received from other agencies and individuals; these are determined by The Executive Committee who meet every month.

CHAPTER 37

As we know, Frank was quite a lover of sport and he was very fond of a game of golf, and he never missed an opportunity to play when it presented itself. He was a participant in a charity match, which was held at Shirley Golf Club, in the Midlands, and was on behalf of The Variety Club of Great Britain. All the proceeds from the tournament were donated to under privileged and handicapped children. Frank was Captain of the Variety Club Golfing Society, amongst other show business personalities taking part were comedian Jasper Carrott, boxers John Conteh and Henry Cooper and footballer Bobby Charlton. It turned out to be a good day for all the players and the spectators seemed to enjoy themselves too.

Frank was regularly asked to carry out cabaret work which he particularly enjoyed. He was asked to work for his old friend George Savva, at Caesars Palace, Luton. He had great respect for Frank and considered him to be a truly international artist. He felt he would have no trouble filling his venue.

George Savva was born in Cornwall but left in 1956 to work in London at the young age of fifteen years. He stayed with friends of his family and was soon offered a job in the catering industry. He worked as a waiter and general dog's body in Cranbourne Street, for the Forte Group, next door to the 'Talk of The Town'. He later went on to work at 'Caesar's Palace' for the grand sum of £25 per week. He worked his way to the top and eventually became manager of the club.

He was there for the next ten years and during that time he arranged for a number of top American performers to appear. These included singers Jack Jones, Frankie Laine, Johnny Mathis and Roy Orbison, as well as Frank and other British artistes. He eventually left and went to work at the Helmen Club, at Usk, Gwent. Eventually this was renamed The Stardust.

In 1978, George was approached by a Mr Pat Cowan, who had purchased a club in London called Blazers. Pat Cowan asked George if he would be prepared to manage the club, which had been left very run down and needed refurbishment. George accepted the offer but it turn out to be a very difficult job. He had to work very long hours, sometimes from eight in the morning until midnight, to get it up and running.

By 1990, George was now in a position to purchase his old club, The Stardust at Usk, which he did. Only three years later George felt that the cabaret scene was dying and decided to call it a day. He and his wife Pam decided to move to Cyprus where he soon found work in the catering business. For a while, they were very happy in Cyprus but were eventually persuaded to return to Britain. Because of his vast experience and very high regard to which he was held, he was asked to manage the Maes Manor Hotel, Gwent, South Wales. Once again, George had an enormous amount of work to do to the hotel. This hotel too had been left to run down and required a lot of work, but he eventually managed to return it to its former glory.

CHAPTER 38

Frank returned to the Liverpool stage in 1969 for the first time in five years. He was to open in "The Frankie Vaughan Spectacular" at the Royal Court Theatre. Also on the same bill was impersonator Mike Yarwood, and comedian Dev Shawn. Whilst rehearsing, Frank's two sons were in the wings watching their father work. David was then aged sixteen and Andrew aged three. The children would be staying in Liverpool with their parents until the end of the show.

Frank was often referred to as 'Mr Entertainment' and was the first British artiste to win the much coveted 'Gold Microphone', which was International Sound Industries premier award to show business. This obviously meant a great deal to a performer. He was delighted to be back as the last time he had appeared in Liverpool was in the pantomime "Puss in Boots" with Jimmy Tarbuck.

Frank was never short of invitations to make appearances either on stage or making an appearance to raise money for worthy causes. A number of them were from local Boys' clubs who he never refused unless he was otherwise engaged. At that time, Frank had helped to raise nearly one million pounds for the various clubs.

During his long career, Frank made many good friends on his travels. Some of his fans even became friends of both him and Stella as they turned up everywhere he appeared and they became very familiar to him. Whenever possible, he would sit and chat with them and eventually learned quite a lot about their lives and their families. Certain acquaintances became long time friends. Two of these friends were Pat and Ralph Hassell.

In 1971, he celebrated his Silver Jubilee year in show business. He was in Derby at 'The Talk of the Midlands' a large entertainment complex. While he was there, he took the opportunity to visit old friends in the Midlands area. These included Pat and Ralph who lived in the Solihull area of the Midlands and who had become very close fiends of Frank and Stella. They had two sons Gary and Alan and a daughter Michelle.

The friendship had begun when Gary and Michelle were working as a double act, and were appearing on the same bill as a young woman singer named Joyce Howard. It was Christmas and although Pat and Ralph were Jewish and kept their own religious days, they also celebrated Christmas with their family.

Joyce was staying in digs in the Midlands during the run of the show. When Pat heard that Joyce would be on her own during Christmas day, she insisted that she must come and have dinner with the family and spend the whole of Christmas day with them. Joyce appreciated the offer very much and had a wonderful time with this very friendly family. That evening Joyce asked if it was possible to watch a show on television as Frankie Vaughan was the star. Pat was only too pleased to agree, as she liked watching Frank too. She asked Joyce if she was a fan of Frankie Vaughan. What a surprise Pat had when Joyce said she was indeed a fan of his as he was married to her sister Stella!

When Joyce told Stella and Frank how kind Pat had been and what a lovely time she had with the Hassell family, Frank telephoned Pat and thanked her for being so kind to Joyce while she was away from home. From that time, Frank and Stella eventually became very good friends with Pat and Ralph. They would stay with them on occasion when in the Midlands and David also was a guest a couple of times. Ralph was a jeweller and owned a number of jewellery shops in the Midlands. Both his sons followed him into the jewellery business, which he taught them - Gary eventually working at Tiffany jewellers in New York.

The two families became such friends that whenever he was appearing in Birmingham or surrounding areas, Frank would stay with Pat and Ralph. He was not fond of staying in hotel rooms by himself as it was very lonely, he much preferred staying with his friends. They made him feel completely at home by treating him as one of the family. Frank became very fond of them and other members of the family; they all enjoyed each other's company. Frank could relax completely at their home and at times he would take it upon himself to invade the kitchen and cook everyone a meal.

CHAPTER 39

Over the years, Pat and Ralph received invitations to family weddings and Bar Mitzvah of Stella and Frank's youngest child Andrew. Also to the Bar Mitzvah of their grandchildren. Always happy occasions.

Frank was staying with Pat and Ralph and expecting his car to be returned after being serviced. When Frank heard someone knocking at the front door, he at first ignored it thinking someone would answer. Everyone was busy at the back of the house, and Pat was cooking a meal. Frank was upstairs and in his dressing gown and slippers after taking a shower. When no one answered the door, he decided he had better answer the door himself.. He opened the door to a young lady who was returning his car. Frank thanked her and asked her how she was getting back home. When she told him she was getting a bus to the train station Frank offered to take her to the station, as it was only a short distance away. He took his keys and jumped in his car as he was, in his dressing gown and slippers.

When he returned to the Hassell's home he rang the bell but had no response. He rang a number of times but still no one came to let him in. He was totally unaware that Pat had switched off the doorbell to prevent him being disturbed by neighbours wanting autographs, which quite often happened when word got around that he was staying. Eventually he had to take drastic action to obtain entry!

When the telephone rang and Pat answered, he said, "I am locked out, please let me in". Pat asked who was speaking, "It's me, Frank," he said. "It can't be Frank, he is upstairs taking a shower" Pat replied. She thought someone was making a joke call. Frank was getting quite irate by now and said "It's me Pat, I am in a telephone box round the corner, I am in my dressing gown and slippers, I am locked out, open the bloody door!" Pat had totally forgotten she had switched off the bell earlier in the day. Of course, the whole family had a good laugh thinking of Frank standing in a telephone box in his dressing gown and slippers.

On another occasion when Frank was staying with the family, Frank had to get to Elmdon airport. This was the old airport for Birmingham long before the International airport was built, and was on the opposite side of the airfield to the terminals that exist today. He was being flown in a small private plane to Glasgow. It was at the time of the Easterhouse project and he was in a hurry to get to Scotland for a meeting, Pat was to drive him to catch his plane.

Frank was always aware when reporters were around. When it was known that he was appearing in the Midlands, the reporters would turn up and sit near to Pat and Ralph's house in the hope of catching him. When they were about to leave the house, Frank became aware of a reporter sitting in his car just a little way from the house. He asked Pat "Can you lose him?" Pat obviously knew the usual route to the airport but also she knew the surrounding areas very well. Off she drove with the reporter following. She took left and right turns here there and everywhere and at last the reporter had to stop for traffic lights. They arrived at the airport with no sign of the him.

As she pulled up at the front of the airport, she was told by a security man that she could not park there. She explained she had Frankie Vaughan with her and he had to catch an urgent flight to Glasgow. When the man bent down and looked in the car he realised she was indeed telling the truth. He smiled at Frank and said, "That's alright then you can stay, do you want to go in with him to see him off, I'll keep an eye on your car?" Frank immediately said "Yes she does" and off they went into the terminal for Frank to board his waiting plane. Pat only stayed long enough to see the little two seater take off and then returned home. On arriving back at her house, she could see the reporter was back and sitting in his car. He walked up to Pat and said "You managed to lose me didn't you and you have taken him to the airport?" Pat said, "No I have not, but as you are still here you had better come in for a cup of tea", typical Pat.

Ralph had a large circle of friends, Frank being one of them. One day they decided to go to the races together. The car park attendant asked who they were. "I'm Frankie Vaughan" said Frank. "I'll need to see your permit", said the attendant. "I'm Ralph Hassell," said Ralph. "Well come in then", said the attendant. Frank and Ralph had a good laugh about it. Ralph loved meeting all sorts of people, and would travel by bus for the joy of meeting his customers on the way. He had no regard for class or position, and enjoyed holding a conversation with anyone he met.

Sadly, Ralph passed away in September 1998. He and Pat had been married for 57 happy years. Having now become friends with Pat and her daughter Michelle, my wife and I can fully understand why Frank enjoyed staying with the family. Pat is a very warm person and instantly made us feel very welcome when we met. We discussed her memories of Frank and briefly looked through the Red Book. She very kindly let us take the book away with us to read, and use any material we found interesting, which we have been so grateful for.

CHAPTER 40

Frank returned to the Midlands a few years later for his thirtieth anniversary in show business. It was held at the Night Out club in Birmingham and recorded by the BBC to be later shown on television. He hardly ever seemed to rest for very long before being on the go once again. He was appearing in Bournemouth for a summer season and on the bill was brilliant comedian Les Dawson who had become a very good friend of Frank. It was almost impossible not to become friends with Les as he was such a friendly down to earth character. He was born in Manchester and began his career as a pianist before deciding he was getting more work as a comedian. He was discovered in 1967 on Opportunity Knocks, the TV talent show. From then on he was seldom off the television. Sadly Les died in June 1993.

After Bournemouth, Frank appeared at the London Palladium for The Royal Variety Show, which was always a coveted engagement for the stars. Like many other stars, Frank quite often received requests for help from a variety of charities. He travelled up and down Britain to carry out appearances and shows for these charities. He enjoyed meeting people from different parts of the country.

He made the decision to try to reduce the amount of cabaret work he was doing. He wanted to spend more time at home with Stella and the children. Continually being away from home was not fair to them, and he missed his family a great deal.

He had an offer to appear in a stage show in London called 42nd Street at Drury Lane. It was a acting and singing role and his West End debut. After much thought, he decided to accept the role as it appealed very much to him. He agreed with his agent, Peter Charlesworth, that he would do the show and the contract was signed. It was a great deal of work as it was something entirely different to his normal shows. Also, it was six nights a week which was very hard work, but he really enjoyed himself. As well as the West End show, he was also doing Sunday night shows at various venues throughout the country.

He was also appearing at the Birmingham Hippodrome where he was doing one show a day. He was asked to increase this to two shows a day, as the demand was so high. Unfortunately, he had to turn this offer down, as it would have been too big a commitment along with 42nd Street. He would not have had any time to spend with his family.

The London show was going well but Frank pulled a tendon in his leg, which was becoming very painful. He carried on working for a while but he then began to develop stomach trouble. At first, he took no notice of this but it became more painful. He still tried to carry on, as he did not want to let down the audiences or the other performers in the show. Eventually, he was forced to give in when he became very ill. He was rushed to hospital where it was discovered that he was suffering from inflammation of the stomach, and peritonitis. He had not realised how ill he had been until it was explained what a narrow escape he had had. Worrying about the show could have cost him his life at the time.

He was touched by the kind messages and good wishes he received, and very grateful to the hospital and the nursing staff for the wonderful care they had given him. He took quite a while to recover, and after he returned home, he needed time to build up his strength. However, when he was well enough to return to the show, he was amazed to find the production company had replaced him in the part of producer, Julian Marsh. Frank was very upset, as he had been lead to believe that he would be returning to the production when he was well. He was very disappointed to lose the part of Julian Marsh.

When he eventually returned to work, he soon realised he was still quite weak and would have to pace himself and take time to recover, after all he had been very ill indeed. He had to be sensible for a while as to the work he accepted. Stella did her best to make him follow medical advice but this was not easy. He found having to slow down very frustrating as he was so used to working at a much faster pace. However, eventually he did recover his strength and could not wait to get on stage once more.

CHAPTER 41

Whenever he returned to his home town of Liverpool, he attracted quite a crowd. Wherever he went everyone wanted to shake his hand. The girls were openly adoring and the men greeted him like a long-lost friend.

He was taking a walk around the old familiar areas one day when Harry, an electricity board workman yelled "Hello" to Frank as he passed. He then said "Tell you what, you're looking younger, and I'll tell you something else - you did a better job of Green Door than this new fella. What's his name - trembling something?" "Shaking Stevens" said Frank with a laugh. "Shaking, he wants shaking" said Harry, "What a load of rubbish".

He walked to the Pier Head, where his grandmother used to take him for Eccles cakes and mugs of tea. An old down and out took Franks hand and said "Hello, Frank old friend". Everyone would acknowledge him.

Frank carried on making his tour of favourite areas, and when he arrived at Devon Street and passed the spot where number 37 had once stood, he stopped to talk to a group of workers in the warehouse which now occupied the site. A middle-aged woman touched his arm and said "You were born here, weren't you?" "That's right" Frank replied "How did you know?" She told him she lived in the house after Frank and his family, and her sons were born there.

His old school in Granby Street was still standing though, and as he entered the playground he was surrounded by children who came running straight into his arms. He once had said how sad he was that so much of Liverpool had been allowed to run down, but the people were exactly as they have always been. When it comes to optimism and quick humour, they are the tops. His fellow Liverpudlians thought he was the tops too.

At a special ceremony at the guildhall in 1983, Frankie Vaughan was awarded the Freedom of the City of London. He was the first former King Rat to be made a Freeman of the City.

CHAPTER 42

Stella and Frank had several good things happen in the 1970s. A week or two after celebrating his twenty five years in show business, he and Stella became grand-parents for the first time. Karen, the wife of his eldest son, David, gave birth to a baby girl.

12 January 1976, Susan, Frank and Stella's daughter, married Paul Sassienie at the synagogue in London's St John's Wood. Among the guests were the comedy duo Morecambe and Wise. Eric, in usual form said, "I have known the bride since before she was borne".

On the 6 June that same year, Stella and Frank celebrated their Silver Wedding Anniversary.

The Birmingham Metropole Hotel was to hold its first International Cabaret and Dinner Dance on 27 of March 1976 in the Palace Suite. Frank was delighted to be asked to provide the cabaret for this initial venture by the Metropole Hotel. The music was supplied by the big band of George Fierstone, and also featured Jo Marney and the Herbie McTaggart Clansmen.

A couple of weeks after his forty ninth birthday in February the following year, his fans had organised a party to celebrate the occasion. The party was held at St Johns Hotel, Solihull. It was the tenth such celebration which had been organised by his fan club, 'Frank and Friends', the official fan club which had more than 1,000 members at that time.

Jackie Salmons of Northampton, chairman of the fan club said "He is just a warm hearted, regular guy, not distant from his fans like some stars". His friend, Pat Hassell was one of the party. She rarely missed an appearance when Frank was playing in the Midlands. After a chorus of "for he's a jolly good fellow", the party headed for Birmingham to see their favourite star in action at the Night Out club.

The following year, Frank released an unusual long playing record. It was some-thing he had wanted to do for a long time, but always something occurred to pre-vent it happening. It was called "Frankie Vaughan 100 Golden Greats". It was unusual in as much as it was recorded in 20 individual medleys, each with its own theme, such as: Moonlight Medley, It's Raining, Sunshine Medley, Love Songs, Johnny Mercer Medley, and so on. Under each heading were listed from four to six songs for each medley.

A great deal of work went into compiling the songs as most of them were quite old and some even went as far back as 1920. This meant that the music sheets for these old songs had to be found. Producer, Gordon Smith patiently and painstakingly leafed through old music books and catalogues to find the music.

Then came the job of arranging them, and this job was undertaken by Al Saxon. He completed this mammoth task in less than one month. They recorded all of these 100 songs in six days. It had been extremely hard work for all concerned but worth it when the double disc LP was finally finished. I have this LP myself and the variation of each medley is very well compiled and a pleasure to listen to even now.

That same year Frank released another album titled 'Seasons For Lovers'. Two songs which appear on the album were written by his son David, which he wrote for his father. These are 'Take Me', and 'Moments', and a third song, 'Seasons For Lovers' the title song, David co-wrote.

In January the following year, Frank was appearing in the Midlands for six nights at the New Cresta Club, Solihull. He would be celebrating his fiftieth birthday the following month. On October 12 of that year he was honoured by the Variety Club of Great Britain with a special luncheon to celebrate his twenty five years in show business.

Frank had always enjoyed performing in different countries even though the travelling was sometimes quite exhausting. In August 1981 he made an appearance in cabaret somewhere he had never been before, that was South Africa. This was at the Calabash club at the Holiday Inn, Maseru. He met the secretary of his fan club, Joy Raphael. Joy had run his fan club in South Africa for a number of years and was sure that he would never make it to Maseru. She and the fans were quite disappointed that Frank was not doing the rounds of various venues at that time, but it gave her great pleasure to be able to have a chat with him.

From the moment he stepped on stage, he had a fantastic reception from the audience of about four hundred. Although there were many young people in the audience, they still seemed to appreciate his older songs. They sang along to numbers like "My Love" and "Cecilia", and included "Garden of Eden" and "Kisses Sweeter Than Wine". His newer releases included "The Road of Life" and "Ragtime Piano Joe", in which his pianist-musical director Roy Hilton was the star. His rousing delivery of his closing number, "Hava Nagila" set the whole place ablaze. This time, the long journey had certainly been worth it.

CHAPTER 43

Frank always managed to do his own golf classic, which he had carried out since 1983. It was held at Hazelmere Golf Club around May or June. All proceeds as usual went to the Boys' Clubs. He also received a donation from his vast fan club, which was nationwide. This eventually became worldwide, having branches in most major cities. All money from the fans was forwarded through his agent, Peter Charlesworth.

A number of celebrities always appeared at these golf classics and a number of them appeared each year.

1994 amongst those appearing were: James Bolam, Ian Botham, Tim Brooke-Taylor, Trevor Brooking, Jess Conrad, Henry Cooper, Cheryl Gillan MP, Jimmy Hill, Geoff Hurst, Dave King, Ian Lavender, Kenny Lynch, Mick McManus, Ray McVay, Lance Percival. Alan Randall, Stan Stennett, Freddie Truman, Marty Wilde and Kenneth Wolstenholme.

1995 Nick Beale, Tim Brooke-Taylor, Mike Burton, Martin Chivers, Jess Conrad, John Conteh, Henry Cooper, Richard Digance, Gareth Hunt, Brian Jacks, Colin Keyes, Dave King, Ian Lavender, Kenny Lynch, Mick McManus, Ray McVay, Pete Murray, Peter Osgood, Alan Randall, Eric Sykes, Jimmy Tarbuck, Marty Wilde and Kenneth Wolstenholme.

1996 Johnnie Briggs, Tim Brooke-Taylor, Mike Burton, Martin Chivers, Dec Clusky, Jess Conrad, Henry Cooper, Cheryl Gillan MP, Joe Goodman, Jimmy Hill, Laurie Holloway, Gareth Hunt, Brian Jacks, Kenny Lynch, Mick McManus, Pete Murray, Ray McVay, Peter Osgood, Lance Percival, Robert Powell, Alan Randall, Eddy Shah, Stan Stennett, Eric Sykes, Marty Wilde, Nigel Winterburn and Kenneth Wolstenholme.

The main purpose of these golf classics was to raise money for the Boys' Clubs and they raised an enormous amount of money over the years, but it also gave everyone involved the opportunity to have a great day out and just enjoy themselves.

CHAPTER 44

In August 1984 Frank spent the day in Nuneaton, Warwickshire. He was to tour most of the town and meet several traders plus people who had won prizes in competitions. Frank was to present these prizes to the winners. One lucky winner was Christine Oliver who won a buffet lunch with Frank from the carvery at the Novotel near Bedworth, Nuneaton. Christine said, "He is a real charmer and just what I expected". The lunch was her prize for winning a 'Fabulous Trader' competition.

Frank did the rounds of many traders that day and officially opened the new indoor market, which had been trading for only two weeks. He also visited Anglian Window Centre, Flair Home Heating and various others throughout the town. The turn out was amazing everywhere he went and a good time was had by everyone.

A local car sales room had provided him with a Montego car for his use while in the town. As he met one army of fans, Frank was surprised when he bumped into a nurse, Alice Guiney who gave him a painful reminder of their last meeting seventeen years previously.

Frank had been appearing at the Coventry theatre in 'Puss in Boots' when he tripped up on stage. He had to be taken to hospital where it was found that he had dislocated his shoulder. When the switch board at the hospital rang through to say that Frankie Vaughan was on his way, Alice was convinced they were pulling her leg as everyone knew that she was a great fan of his. When he arrived in Alice's department, she couldn't believe it was really Frankie Vaughan. She asked him how he came by his injury and they had quite a chat which made Alice's day.

After Puss In Boots, he continued with his cabaret appearances which were always very popular and much in demand. One appearance was at Caesar's nightclub in Luton. He was again working with his old friend club manager George Savva who always considered Frank to be a truly international artist. Most top artistes from the USA appeared at Caesar's, and George always made sure everything was in order, and at its best for the stars.

Frank was asked by the BBC to narrate a programme on Al Jolson's life at the forty-year anniversary of Al's death. As he was a big fan of the singer, he was very pleased to oblige. He really enjoyed the broadcast as he sang many of the songs from that era in his early career. He was also asked to sing on BBC's "Friday Night is Music Night" at Fairfield Hall, London. where he was accompanied by his Musical Director, Ivor Raymonde.

He was once again in Birmingham for a Sunday night show at the Odeon cinema, again with a full house. He performed in Birmingham yet again in December 1989 at the Alexander Theatre. This was to launch a major national tour with a show called 'Swing Into Christmas'.

Fred Norris, the theatre critic interviewed Frank, who spoke of the early days, when he did shows at the Windsor Club, Bearwood, also Dudley Hippodrome. He always said that so much of his show business life had centred in and around Birmingham and the Midlands, he was pleased that people still came to see him. The cast of the show included Stutz Bear Cats, Patti Gold and The New Squadronaires orchestra. After the tour, which was a great success, Frank and Stella had a much-needed holiday in Spain. He returned to work in a show for George Savva at Blazers night club, Windsor.

For some time Frank had concentrated more on cabaret work than making new records. However, in 1984 he released a new single called 'Dreamers'. It was taken from a musical about tragic Hollywood star Jean Seberg. She was an American actress who played the role of Joan of Arc in the film 'Saint Joan'. She stared in 34 films in Hollywood and France but sadly took her own life at the age of forty in Paris. Dreamers brought Frank back into the record scene once again.

CHAPTER 45

Frank occasionally did shows on cruise ships, one particular cruise was going to Sweden. On board were a party from Australia who had hardly heard of Frank at that time. As usual, he made the rounds of the cabaret room in between singing and saying "hello" to old and new fans. The whole show was pure magic with everyone so relaxed and happy by the time they retired.

The next morning Frank did an autograph and photograph session. The fans always loved these sessions as it was an easygoing get together which was always great fun. There was great deal of laughter and everyone enjoyed chatting with Frank. A donation of fifty pence was asked for each signed photograph. By the time it was over, sixty pounds had been collected as a donation for the Boys' Clubs.

At this time, BBC Birmingham used to host a chat show called Pebble Mill at One and Frank was one of their guests. To mark the arrival of the Good Old Days stage show, each guest or presenter was dressed in clothes of the 1901 period. Presenter Paul Cola wore a false moustache, which made him itch, and all the guests including Frank, comedian Norman Vaughan, and Leonard Sachs were stars of the show, which was running at the Birmingham Hippodrome Theatre at the time.

Spring 1985, Frank, Stella and her mother Mrs Shock, had a wonderful holiday in Miami. They spent one week with their daughter Susan, which was a real treat for them all. Susan was working on the Caribbean cruise liner at the time and was delighted to spend time with her mother, father and grandmother.

Frank also was due to start work on two different cruise ships. One was a mini cruise to Denmark. Stella was able to join him and many of his fans were booked on the cruise. It was to last just a few days from the first to the third of March. Then the Bombay to Cape Town leg of the QE2 world cruise from 17 to 28 March. Stella always enjoyed meeting the fans whenever she could and they were always very friendly towards her. There was a great deal lot of laughing and joking between them all.

Frank's engagements for the next few months were:

5 March	**Holiday Trek programme - Channel 4 TV**
8 March	**Charity Show at the Kings Hall, Ilkley**
10 March	**Charity Show at the London Palladium**
14 March	**Mecca Social Club, Essex Road, London**
13 April	**Alfred Beck Centre, Hayes (2 shows)**
19 April	**Scotch Corner Hotel, Nr. Darlington**
2 May	**Whose Baby - Thames Television**
4 August	**Cliffs Pavilion, Southend-on-Sea (2 shows)**
9 August	**Princes Theatre, Clacton-on-Sea (2 shows)**
25 August	**Princess Theatre, Hunstanton, Norfolk (2 shows)**

He was returning to Hunstanton by popular demand.

This was just a small part of Frank's working year, but an example of the type of schedule which he carried out quite regularly.

In 1988, Frank was bestowed with a great honour. He became very emotional when he was made an Honorary Fellow of the City's Polytechnic in an award ceremony at Liverpool Cathedral. He was wearing a beautiful cap and gown, which had been made especially for him.

Frank was reduced to tears and apologised to everyone for becoming so emotional. He said he was truly honoured to receive such a very special degree. He paid tribute to his family and friends for their support. The polytechnic records said fellowships only went to the proud sons and daughters of Merseyside who had risen to the top of their professions while serving the community.

February 1988 when Frank reached his sixtieth birthday, an article appeared in the Jewish Gazette covering his life to date.

CHAPTER 46

A celebration was organised for February 1990, to mark not only Frank's sixty second birthday, but also his fortieth anniversary in show business. A cabaret had been organised which included the Kaye Sisters who had become good friends with Frank since making records with him.

'Frank and Friends' presented Frank and Stella with an album to mark "40 Years in Show Business" containing many photographs taken at 'Frank and Friends' functions over the last 22 years. The first "Frankie Vaughan Stars", telegrams received at the Celebration Party in Derby for the 25 years in show business, and finally, letters of tribute to Frank from the National Association of Boys' Clubs, Grand Order of Water Rats, Lord Spencer and H.R.H. The Duke of Gloucester. These read as follows:

From the National Director of the Association of Boys' Clubs:

All your friends at the NABC join with me in sending you our very sincere congratulations and best wishes upon your completion of 40 years in show business. You have over that time given endless pleasure to millions of people and it is fitting that this important milestone in your stage career be marked this evening.

It is also fitting for us to recall that you have been associated with the Boys' Club Movement for 35 years during which time you have raised, in various ways, hundreds of thousands of pounds for the Boys' Club Movement and done so much to publicise the work which is carried out by our many clubs throughout the country. Undoubtedly, the title "Mr Boys' Clubs" is most aptly conferred upon you. From your thousands of friends in the Boys' Club Movement, I send sincere and very best wishes.

Derek Harris - National Director

From King Rat-David Lodge and all his Brother Water Rats

For the past thirty years it has been our good fortune that Frankie Vaughan has been a devoted brother of our Grand Old Order. In 1968 he received the highest accolade possible from his fellow performers - that of being elected King Rat. It is, therefore, our great pleasure to send him fraternal greetings on this special occasion in celebration of his birthday and Forty Years as a great entertainer.

With love from King Rat David Lodge & all his Brother Water Rats

Lord Spencer of Althorp

It seems hardly possible for us who know him well to accept the fact that he has been in Show Business for 40 years. His youthfulness and zest for living make that difficult to believe.

He has always given so much of himself to his audiences and to his admirers all over the world. But it is the young men and boys of this country who owe him the most.

For many years he has been a pillar of strength to the Boys' Club movement, with his vitality giving a lead to the boys' varied activities and, by example, giving high standards of decency and integrity which will have been followed by boys in many parts of the country.

Frank had done great work for his profession, while his continuing influence among a host of boys and young men has been thoroughly wholesome and beneficial. Well done Frank!

**From Kensington Palace from H.R.H. The Duke of Gloucester
President of National Association of Boys' Clubs.**

Congratulations to Frankie Vaughan on the 40 years that he has entertained the public so successfully and also many thanks for the great and valued support that he has given to many friends and admirers in the Boys' Clubs during that period.

Many of his fellow performers and friends wanted to celebrate this milestone with him. One very cleverly arranged tribute was from George Savva from his club in Usk, Gwent where Frank had performed in the past. George wrote:

Sorry we cannot be there. At first, we thought, "There must be a way" but no, I am afraid our presence is required in Usk. But we feel sure you will enjoy dancing the night away, with friends and family, they can give you their gifts and you can "Give them the Moonlight". Give our kind regards to Stella, she has always been a "Tower of Strength" and if you see "Dolly" say "Hello". Another Happy Birthday goes to show that your "Life is a Cabaret" so may your party start off in tune and continue in harmony.

Fondest Love from Pam, George, Roddy and all the old pro's at Usk

The following poem was sent by Denis Eldridge:
The Husband of the Housewife who belongs to 'Frank and Friends'

In our house there is a suitcase the largest one can buy
I can hardly lift it and here's the reason why
It's full of paper cuttings, programmes, tickets and the like
Going back to Brighton '57 when we first saw Frank at the mike
There are also scrapbooks and photographs by the score
Autographs by the hundred and still she queues for more
Then of course there are the records, singles, EP's and LPs
Plus tapes of these same records, some old 78's but no CDs
We also have a 'phone in our house, just like in any other
To keep us all in constant touch, you're not kidding brother!
Jackie rings, SIR's coming down, just got the latest date
Did you know that you've been knighted by Queen Jackie mate?
Panic stations, ring theatre, book the whole front row
Hubby dear write out a cheque or I know they all will go
Contact all her fellow fans with this latest piece of news
They all get the message, I get the telephone blues
I listen to discussions on what clothes to wear
The price of the tickets, where to meet, appointments for their hair
I hear it over and over, I want to scream and shout
If you don't get off that 'phone I'll have it taken out
But I don't, why? 'cos I'm a coward, a forgiving sort of guy
I do my best to understand but I really can't think why
I'll even forgive you Frank if what I've heard is true
That you're thinking of retiring at the age of sixty two
But lastly on a serious note, there are many compensations
Just look around at all the friends we meet on these occasions
Please 'Frank and Friends' let's drink a toast to SIR and his wife Stella
He's put up with us for all these years and he's a smashing fella!

After the celebrations, a Souvenir Special Edition of Frank and Friends news
letter was sent to members to congratulate Frank on a wonderful evening of
celebrations. Included in the letter was a Birthday Times for Friday, February 3
1928. This listed various headings of what was happening on that day when Frank
was born. Included was Tunes of the Times such as, Button Up Your Overcoat, I
Wanna Be Loved By You, Can't Help Lovin' Dat Man, I Can't Give You
Anything But Love, Carolina Moon, When You're Smiling, My Blue Heaven to
name but a few.

People Who Share Your Birthday such as Felix Mendelssohn-Composer 1809, Val Doonican-Singer, and Doris Speed, Actress. The Prime Minister at that time was Stanley Baldwin and Opposition Leader was David Lloyd George.

A month after these celebrations Frank was back hard at work and looking forward to the following few months of engagements. From Saturday the first of March, he had a full diary. He was appearing at The Playhouse, Epsom where he did two shows, 6 pm and 8.45 pm. Thursday March 22 The Daily Star Gold Star Awards Lunch at the Savoy Hotel.

April

4	**MacIntyre Charity Golf tournament at Woburn**
5	**Jimmy Hill Golf Day for Fulham Football Club at Harewood Downs**
7	**Attending the Easter Ball in aid of Boys' Clubs at Stowe School, Buckingham**
8	**"Highway" with Harry Secombe**
25	**Celebrity Guild Golf at Dyrham Park**
26	**Frankie Vaughan to present award at the federation of British Audio Awards Dinner at the Royal Lancaster Hotel, London**

May

3	**Boys' Clubs of Wales Golf Tournament at Porthcawl.**
24	**Roy Thompson Hall, Toronto, Canada**
25	**" " " " "**

August

22	**Frankie Vaughan Golf Classic at Hazlemere Golf and Country Club,**

October

13	**Secombe Centre, Sutton - 2 shows**

It is easy to see how little free time Frank had from one month to the other. He was so used to being busy and truly enjoyed both his charity work and his performances.

CHAPTER 47

It was 1992, the year after losing our son Simon, when I decided to try to contact Peter Charlesworth who was Frankie Vaughan's agent. I wanted to try to raise as much money as possible to help people suffering mental illness. I was about to ask if it was possible for Frank to appear in a show on behalf of National Schizophrenia Fellowship (NSF). As it happened, he was appearing in a charity show at The Theatre Royal, Windsor with Roy Castle. This was in aid of Cancer Research, and the proceeds would go towards buying a scanner. A Consultant from the cancer hospital was selling the tickets. His name was Mr Justin Johnson.

I spoke with Mr Johnson, and explained my involvement in raising money for this particular charity. He was very understanding as he knew how difficult it was for money to be raised. He offered to forward a letter from me, to Davy Kaye, who was a friend of Frank and also a member of the Grand Order of Water Rats. Mr Kaye then very kindly passed my letter on to Frank.

Shortly afterwards, I received a reply from Frank's secretary, Barbara Langston, offering Frank's sympathy for our loss. My request would be forwarded to his agent Mr Peter Charlesworth, who would contact me direct. I received a letter very soon asking what I had in mind. I was quite honest with him that I had no experience in organising such a large show, and certainly not with such a high calibre star as Frankie Vaughan.

I sent the relevant details in writing as requested by Mr Charlesworth and I received confirmation of the booking. Everything would be arranged through his London office. I found Peter Charlesworth very helpful throughout.
As things progressed, I received a letter from Frank saying how pleased he was that everything was going well with the arrangements for the show, and that he was only too pleased to help. Also, if my wife and I attended any of his shows we were to make ourselves known to him.

Frank was appearing in Blackpool for the 1992 summer season at the North Pier. My wife and I stayed over night in Blackpool, and went to see the show. We told the theatre manager about the letter from Frank, and during the interval, we were asked backstage to meet both Stella and Frank. It was the first time we had met them in person, but they were both most kind. He said he was very pleased to meet us, and no matter what happened he would be there for our charity show.

We gave them a framed painting of a ballerina, which had been painted by our son Simon. We knew that Frank was interested in art from his younger days. He commented that Simon was a brilliant artist, and that the detail was very fine. Stella said it was very sad that Simon had left us at such a young age. I am afraid that I got quite emotional, but did not feel embarrassed because as parents, they both understood.

I kept in touch with Peter Charlesworth, who said he would help in any way he could. I have to say, at that time I needed help. I made arrangements for the show to take place at The Chesford Grange Hotel in Kenilworth, Warwickshire. This was a cabaret venue where Frank had made an appearance in the past. All the local press were kind enough to advertise the show, which was set for 25 November 1992.

Everything was going well, and true to his word, Peter Charlesworth was very supportive. The tickets were selling very well, and would have sold out by November. People from all over the country were asking for tickets. This made me realise just how popular and how large a following Frank had. His British fan club was vast. Ticket sales were down to me and newspaper advertising, as the venue was not allowed to sell tickets for charity shows. Many of our friends and family also bought tickets and everyone was looking forward to a great night.

Unexpectedly, a situation occurred which no one could have foreseen. Frank was in his tenth week of his summer show in Blackpool. He was taking a short break and whilst in Preston playing a game of golf with his brother in law, he took a swing at the ball, and felt a sudden pop in his back. For a short time, he lost all movement in both arms. His brother in law drove him back to the house, which they were renting for the season. Stella was out shopping at the time. Frank had a shower, which seemed to help. He had had two rather bad colds during the past few weeks but thought nothing of it and carried on with the show. His back was still not quite right and he decided to go a physiotherapist. After five days this had not helped to any degree. Stella and Frank were due back home for the Jewish New Year and he always made sure he did not accept any work at this time.

CHAPTER 48

On 6 October, I received a telephone call from Peter Charlesworth to tell me that Frank was not well. He said he would be grateful if I did not disclose it, as the press knew nothing about it. This was followed by a letter to let me know that because Frank's condition had not improved, he would not be well enough to carry out the booking for my charity show on 25 November.

Frank decided to go to his own GP, but Stella insisted he go to the Chilton Hospital where he received excellent attention. This included being given a scan, which appeared to be clear.

They went home to celebrate with his family and friends. As they were enjoying their meal, Frank remembered that his phone was still diverted to Blackpool where he had been working. He switched it back to home, and it rang almost instantly. The hospital in Wycombe had been trying to reach him for hours. The scan which had been taken previously had been sent to John Radcliffe hospital in Oxford, which is well known for specialist treatment. It was found that he had an aneurysm of the main artery, and he was to go immediately to the hospital.

Frank asked if he could finish his meal as he was with friends and family but was told no, and under no circumstance must he drive himself. His brother in law drove both Frank and Stella to the hospital. They were met on arrival by a surgeon, Mr Stephen Westaby, and the situation was explained to them. Frank would have to stay in hospital for the next week while they tried drugs to stabilise his condition. Of course, Frank being his usual self asked if he could go back to finish the show. It was explained to him that this was not possible in his condition.

Everything available was tried for the next five days, to no avail. There was no choice but to operate. It was a major operation, which had to be completed in no more than 30 minutes. The main artery had to be clamped off while the operation was in progress. If it took longer, it could cause paralysis in the patient. Owing to the skill of the surgeon, the operation was completed in the record time of twenty minutes.

To the relief of all concerned, Frank had come through his ordeal. Four days after the operation, Stella wheeled him round the hospital grounds. He told the press he had been sitting on a time bomb, and must be the luckiest man alive. He was well enough to return home by the end of October 1992.

Frank wrote expressing his deep regret for having to let me down. I understood that there was nothing he could do about such a situation and was only glad that he was now on the mend. I did have an offer from Derek Salberg, the then owner of the Alexander theatre in Birmingham. He was willing to ask Les Dawson if he would fill in for Frank, but it would have caused a number of problems including the tickets having to be reprinted. I decided it was too short notice and therefore, I decided to cancel the show. The management at Chesford Grange were most kind, and returned all monies paid for the hire of the venue.

My main concern was for Frank, Stella and their family. It had been a big ordeal for them all. Of course, it was in the press regarding his illness. Stella was inundated with letters, and get-well cards, to such a degree that she had to asked his fans not to send flowers or cards to the hospital, as it put extra work on the staff. Everyone knew that all the kindness was gratefully appreciated by Frank, Stella, and their family.

I received a letter from Frank in March 1993, letting me know he was getting on very well. He was starting to make a few personal appearances on radio, and television. Shortly afterwards, I recall seeing him on a breakfast show with Gloria Hunniford's late daughter, Caron.

Needless to say, it was a very difficult time for Frank after such a major operation. The British Heart Foundation was a great help. He also attended a unit, which helped him regain his strength. This was by doing the right kind of exercise, and taking daily walks. In fact, he went too far on one occasion with Stella's nephew; she thought that they had gotten lost. By the time they arrived home, they had been gone for two hours.

CHAPTER 49

Frank and Stella had kept in touch with Stephen Westaby. During one of their conversations, the surgeon mentioned a conference he had attended in South Africa with the Christian Barnard Foundation. He learned of a young boy who had been in a very severe fire, and was badly burned. His voice box was almost destroyed. His mother was also injured but, even more distressing, his father had perished in the fire.

The surgeon said he was willing to help the boy, but finance was the problem. He would be able to stay in the hospital, and do the operation, but needed an open ended plane ticket. This would enable him to stay as long as necessary to attend to the boy after surgery.

Stella asked how much was needed. She contacted the Curtis family, who were friends of Frank and Stella. They in turn contacted Julia Morley, wife of Eric Morley. Eric was Mecca's general manager of dancing and was made director in 1953. He popularised bingo which was played at Mecca venues throughout the United Kingdom. Julia Morley very kindly made an approach to the Variety Club Special Case team. They were only too pleased to help, and paid for the surgeon to stay in a hotel for as long as necessary.

South African television covered the story. The operation went very well, and the young boy had a new voice box and windpipe. This allowed him to eat normally again. When he was well enough, he sent Stella and Frank a lovely photograph to say how grateful he and his mother were to everyone who helped him. Whilst being interviewed on the late John Dunn show, the story of the young boy was mentioned. Frank became quite emotional when he explained the details of how it all came about.

Frank was the subject of "This Is Your Life" on BBC television, with Michael Aspel, who was also presenter of Antiques Roadshow. Michael had taken over presenting "This Is Your Life" after the death of long time presenter, Eamonn Andrews in 1987.

Frank was recovering from his first aneurysm and hoping to regain his strength and fitness by using the gymnasium. He was taken completely by surprise when in walked Michael Aspel with the Red Book.

Knowing that the tribute was to Frank, when asked, a number of celebrities were very pleased to appear. Jimmy Tarbuck spoke of how Frank had shown him how to fish. Jimmy was quick to tell everyone that he caught a large trout, but Frank decided to take it home, even had the cheek to cook it and eat it himself.

In addition, Ernie Wise made everyone laugh. Morecambe and Wise usually tried to play tricks on their guests and Frank was no exception, but Frank turned the table on them. He arranged for a solicitor to send them a letter saying that he, Frank, intended to sue them for defamation of character, and ruining his career. Ernie asked his forgiveness, and told Frank to keep making the 78rpm records.

The surgeon, Stephen Westaby also appeared, and spoke of the time when he carried out Frank's operation. He said some of his nurses had looked under the sheet whilst Frank was under sedation. Frank pretended to be shocked and replied that he would not appear in his theatre again! Frank then became very serious and told the Stephen Westaby and the audience he could never repay the surgeon for saving his life. Mr Westaby said that Frank had shown great calmness through the whole ordeal. Maybe it was down to all the years of appearing on stage.

A big surprise was in store for Frank and it was a very happy moment for him when Natalie, Stella and Frank's granddaughter, came walking onto the stage. She had travelled from Leeds University to be with her grandfather for this special tribute to him.

The Kaye Sisters were also on the show, as they had made a record with Frank called "Got to have something in the bank, Frank". It sold two hundred and fifty thousand copies. Frank donated all his royalties from this record to the Boys' Clubs. When the Kaye Sisters heard about this, they agreed to donate their percentage of the royalties to the same cause as they and Frank had been friends for a good number of years. Although they were called 'sisters' the Kaye Sisters were not actually related but were three young friends. They were actually Carol Lindsey Young, Shirley Palmer and Sheila Jones.

They went to enormous trouble to present themselves as identical to each other. They had their blonde hair cut in a fringe style and wore identical dresses with wide skirts and very fluffy underskirts which made the skirts stick out. This style was very popular in the fifties. They took their name from their manager, a girl called Carmen Kaye whose determination got them started.

Their popularity started to wane during the 1960s although they still appeared in cabaret up until the late seventies. However, like their rivals the Beverley Sisters, they managed to re-establish themselves much later as a nostalgia act, and once more found themselves in cabaret.

CHAPTER 50

When Frank returned to the Grand Theatre, Wolverhampton for a week in a tribute show for Variety, he was in fine form.

He attended a memorial service that was being held for the late forces favourite Anne Shelton. Frank was one of many stars to attend. Anne had been all over the front line in world war two, to sing for the troops. Although she was not personally associated with this particular song, Frank sang "All The Way" which was her favourite. He had sung it the last time they appeared on a show together at Buckingham Palace and Anne had loved to hear Frank sing this particular song. The London Corpus Christi church was full to overflowing with show people.

Anne was a much-loved singer who was well known for touring Army, Navy and Air Force bases. She was born in South London and in 1942 had her own radio program, 'Calling Malta', which remained on air for around five years. In 1944, she was invited to sing with the Glenn Miller Orchestra. Glenn had a wonderful mellow sound to his music and was very popular during the war years and for a long time after. Glenn asked Anne to stay on with the band and travel to Versailles, France for a series of shows. Unfortunately, she had to turn this down due to other commitments in Britain. It turned out to be very fortunate for her as Glenn Miller's plane was lost over the English Channel shortly afterwards.

Anne also sang with Bing Crosby on the radio show 'Variety Bandbox' and afterwards played a show together singing a duet on the songs "Easter Parade" and "I'll Get By". In 1990, Anne was awarded the OBE for her work with the "Not Forgotten Association", a charitable organization for disabled former service personnel from all wars. She died 31 July 1994.

Once again, Frank went on the fund raising trail. This was to help raise funs for a pioneering project into electrical heart transplants. With a lot of help from his friends, he managed to raise £750,000. The surgeon Simon Westaby, who had operated on Frank, carried out an operation on a Mr Abel Goodman, who was fitted with an electronic heart. Everything went extremely well and he celebrated his 64th birthday a day after the operation.

Each year Frank celebrated his birthday by holding a party, where a number of fans would attend. One of his parties was held at Hazelmere Country Club, Buckinghamshire where he played golf. My wife and I were invited to this through his fan club "Frank and Friends". Quite a number of Frank's fans usually attended. Frank would stand up and tell stories of different amusing incidences involving himself, and at times, Stella too. One of the stories he told at this particular party, was how he was sitting at home reading his Sunday newspaper, when Stella decided she would like to go to a car boot sale which she had heard of. He had never been to one; however, he always did as he was told!

Stella was more than pleased when she spotted a box set of Frank's records, and decided to buy them. He never kept any of his records at home. As they were leaving, Stella tried to take a short cut by climbing over a wall. She slipped, and cut her leg quite badly. Frank drove her to High Wycombe hospital where her injured leg was attended to. Frank went outside on the steps waiting for Stella. He was waiting patiently when a woman ran up to him shouting, "Where the hell have you been? I telephoned for a taxi over an hour ago". She suddenly realised who he was, and they both had a good laugh about it. They chatted for a few minutes and when Stella returned, she and Frank gave the woman a lift to her home. She would have had a good story to tell her family and friends.

These birthday celebrations of Frank's were always very jolly occasions, made even more enjoyable by the fact that both Frank and Stella made their way round the room chatting to everyone on each table. They seemed to be genuinely enjoying themselves and treated everyone as friends, it was a truly lovely day out. Also at the party was Stella's mother, Mrs Shock who is a real character. She started telling everyone comic things about Frank, some of them quite hilarious and we all had a good laugh, at Frank's expense of course! She also said she would like plastic surgery, and that there would be enough skin left over to make a handbag! She was a wonderful fun loving lady.

It was a great day, and during conversation with Frank's secretary, Barbara Langston, it was mentioned that Frank was to appear at Bodelwyddan Castle, near Llandudno, Wales. It was owned by Warner Leisure, and was to launch their first actual hotel complex. Until then, Warner had been known for coastal resorts.

My wife and I attended the launch at Bodelwyddan Castle. A large number of his British fans were there and Frank, as usual, gave a great performance. This was to lead to a great many appearances for Frank at various Warner hotels throughout the country. The shows which we attended, were always completely sold out, in fact one we were unable to attend for this reason.

Frank was never short of requests to appear, and seemed always to be busy. He went on to appear at Brighton Royal Theatre, also the Green Room Café Royal, in London.

He travelled to Derby to perform in the fiftieth Anniversary of the end of the Second World War. It was held at Derby City football ground. My wife and I attended with Joan and Wilf Barker. Joan was secretary of the Coventry branch of 'Frank and Friends' at that time. Judy and I took Ben our six-year-old grandson with us and he had a great time and tried to join in the singing.

It was a fantastic day out. The band was The Squadronaires and Chas and Dave were also on the bill. They were pianist Chas Hodges and guitarist Dave Peacock. They later teamed up with drummer Mick Burt but eventually went out on their own as Chas and Dave the Cockney duo. They wrote and recorded witty songs about life in London and were very popular around the British rock scene of the 1960s and 70s. They are still popular today recording their songs for release on CD. The weather on the day of the concert could not have been more beautiful. The show was a complete sell out and we all had a wonderful time.

Frank was appearing once again in cabaret for Warners at Holme Lacy House, Herefordshire. Once again it was a full house. Every performance was a great experience for the audience. Frank always had an amazing amount of time for his fans, and seemed to thoroughly enjoy himself too. During the following years as Warner opened more holiday hotels, Frank appeared in most of them. They are all beautiful old stately homes which have been totally refurbished and sympathetically extended to accommodate many more guests. As they all have a large cabaret room, they are ideal for popular performers, such as Frank, to appear.

CHAPTER 51

The year of 1993 would be a year to remember for Frank, Stella and all the family. Lord Cottesloe recommended Frank for Deputy Lieutenant of Buckinghamshire. Frank was very pleased but had no idea what this would involve. It had to be agreed by Her Majesty the Queen but no objection was raised and on 14 June 1993, Frank became officially OBE DL. He would be the first entertainer to hold this office. It is an exclusive commission, only given to people with a long-standing record of military or public service. Frank received it for his considerable charity work.

Lord Tavistock, another Deputy Leutenant, was only too pleased to enlightened Frank on the responsibilities of the position. The presentation took place at the home of Commander Fremantle. There were no formal speeches, and Frank commented afterwards that it seemed a very English occasion. The title is for life, and it meant a great deal to him and his family. He said it was not bad for a Northern lad, who came to London with only a five-pound note in his pocket.

Frank was deeply saddened when he heard of the death of the dearly loved comic and very good friend, Les Dawson. He wrote a letter to Tracy, Les's widow, offering his condolences. When Frank was interviewed after his own serious health problems, he said he felt very lucky to be given more time. He was determined to use the opportunity to carry on entertaining his audience, and raising money for his charities.

A very good friend of Stella and Frank, Illa Kodicek, who was a Czech émigré, passed away and left Frank a number of valuable paintings. When they went to auction at Christies of London, they sold for somewhere around £3,000,000. Frank and Stella had no hesitation in giving all proceeds from the sale to the Boys' Clubs.

When the great Joe Loss died in June 1990, an official tribute was held at the Birmingham Hippodrome in October that year. It was in the presence of the Earl and Countess of Shrewsbury, and all proceeds were to be given to Age Concern. Film star, Richard Todd was compere, and Frank was top of the bill. He drove from Newcastle on Tyne with Stella, where he had finished a week in cabaret. When he was first starting out in show business, Frank worked with bands that played as support to Joe Loss who was the main band on the bill. Joe was always very encouraging to Frank. Both Stella and he became great friends with Joe and his wife, Mildred.

Music was to be provided by the Joe Loss Orchestra. Also on the bill was Vince Hill, who had sung on the QE2 accompanied by Joe Loss. The full orchestra and vocalist Rose Brennan, always gave great support to the artistes. Joe was given an OBE in June 1990.

Joe was born 22 June 1909 to Joshua Alexander Loss of Israel and Ada Loss, Russian Jews. His father was a cabinet-maker who had an office furnishing business. Joe started violin lessons at the age of seven and was educated at the Jews' Free School, Trinity College of Music and the London College of Music.

When in 1989 Joe became too ill to travel he entrusted the leadership to Todd Miller, who has led the orchestra through to the present day. Todd had joined the orchestra in 1972 and has continued the great tradition of performing the best in live entertainment for all generations from the big band era to today's charts. Since 1930 the orchestra has never been disbanded and reformed, only new members have replaced those who have passed away. The band has been in constant operation throughout the world.

I can personally recommend this wonderful orchestra as my wife and I went to see them perform a few months ago at our local theatre. Both the players and the singers were superb. It was a marvellous night with a good amount of camaraderie between the players. We are very much looking forward to seeing them again later this year, as they are booked for a return show.

CHAPTER 52

Frank was back once more in cabaret at Holme Lacy House, Hereford. Whenever he was in cabaret at these hotels, they were always fully booked well in advance. Wherever he appeared, it was guaranteed to draw a large following from his 'Frank and Friends Club', as well as many other admirers. As usual, he gave a first class performance, and ended by taking four curtain calls.

One appearance at Holme Lacy House had to be cancelled, as Frank was unwell. Judy and I had booked the weekend there to see Frank and of course we were very disappointed, but Vince Hill stepped in to Frank's spot at short notice and was very well received. He gave a great performance.

Next on Frank's agenda was his yearly golf classic at Hazelmere Golf and Country Club. These annual golf classics always were well attended and large sums of money were raised over the years for the National Association of Boys' Clubs. They also gave a great deal of pleasure to both players and audience. Another donation was made when friends of Frank and Stella left them £14,000, which they also donated to the Boys' Clubs.

Frank was presented with his CBE, in 1997 for his hard work in raising much needed funds to support such organisation. He was proud to receive such an outstanding award, which was presented to him by Prince Charles. As he was making the presentation Prince Charles asked if he was still gargling with the port, it was a previous joke between them. At the event, Frank noticed that the Duke of Edinburgh, who is a companion rat, was not wearing his rat emblem in his lapel. It is meant to be worn at all times. Frank
pointed this out, but the Duke lifted his lapel with a smile to reveal the emblem. He was wearing it on the underside of his lapel. The next time Frank met him he, was wearing it on his vest.

February 1998 was a milestone for Frank. Stella reserved a table at The Savoy, London. It was a dinner dance in the River Room where a trio was playing and a surprise for Frank's seventieth birthday. Once the musicians recognised Frank and Stella, they played Frank's, music most of the evening. He and Stella danced to "Hello Dolly," and at the end of the evening they were last to leave. As they were leaving, the band played "Give Me The Moonlight".

BBC Radio 2 recorded an interview with Frank to mark his birthday. It was transmitted on Sunday 8 February 1998, five days after his birthday. He was also made 'Honorary Fellow' of John Moores University Liverpool, and also received a 'Special Award' at the Liverpool Echo's Arts and Entertainment Awards. That year he also received a BAFTA Lifetime Achievement Award.

During the year, Frank was made 'King Rat' for the second time. This was in recognition of the fantastic amount of money he had raised for charity. Once again he was honoured to hold this title as it was bestowed on him by his fellow Water Rats. It was also a privilege to hold the post for a second term. On the last Lodge night of Frank's reign, two new Baby Rats were inaugurated. These new were musician Rick Wakeman and comedian Joe Pasquale.

Frank's oldest sister Phyllis made the journey from New York for the Water Rats Ball. Frank loved all his sisters but he adored Phyllis. She was determined to be there despite the fact that she was suffering badly from cancer. Earlier that year she'd had a very serious operation and was far from well. However, she was very proud of Frank, and wanted to be with him on this special night. She managed to be at the ball and it was a wonderful evening. All the family went back to Frank and Stella's home afterwards and drank champagne. Shortly afterwards, Phyllis returned home to New York.

Frank had a wonderful year as King Rat. It had been 30 years since he last held this post but it was still as important to him as the first time in 1968.

In October 1998 Frank performed once more at Bodelwyddan Castle, North Wales, again for Warner Holidays. As usual, he gave a great performance, but this was to be his last performance for the Warner Organisation.

The following year saw Frank doing what he loved best, helping other people. He was asked to open a new workshop on behalf of the National Society of Epilepsy. The workshop was in Chalfont St Peters and over 100 supporters were at the unveiling of the new building. It helped two businesses, printers and bookbinders, and also a packaging service. Spokeswoman, Jo Lawrence- King thanked Frank for his great support of this and other local causes, and said he was always very keen to meet the residents. He took a real interest in what their work entailed.

A request was sent to Frank's fan club by the Sands Youth Club in High Wycombe. Jackie Salmons who was secretary of Frank's international fan club, paid a visit to the Sands. She found that the club had no heating whatsoever and arranged for a donation of £550 to be made towards the cost of installation. The donation was from "Frank and Friends" and Mr Peter Boyle, County Director of the Youth Club, wrote expressing his grateful thanks.

In March 1999, Frank did a big concert in Manchester for his daughter's children's school, for charity. They had booked the University Hall, and it was a complete sell out.

However, by April, Frank began to feel unwell. He was due to appear in a special show for the late Lord Lew Grade on the eighteenth of the month. This was to be for invited guests only including professionals from all over the world. The show was held at the Prince of Wales Theatre, London. Frank was a firm believer that if you gave your word you must keep it, therefore he carried out this commitment. He really was not well enough to attend but was determined to keep his promise. Knowing that Frank was very ill, Stella and the family were all waiting in his room.

Frank said how privileged he felt to be there and to be asked to sing for Lew's widow, Kathy. He sang in Yiddish, 'Mandl un Rozshinke' which translates to 'Almonds and Raisins', a Jewish lullaby which has a beautiful haunting melody.

CHAPTER 53

On 23 April, Frank attended a stag lunch at Grosvenor House Hotel, London on St Georges Day. He had quite a shock when he received a standing ovation from some one thousand five hundred men. He blew them a kiss, which they all had a good laugh at. On the 14 May, Frank and Stella attended a dinner at Woburn Abbey Sculpture Gallery. It was for the BABC for young people. Later that month, Frank hosted the Frankie Vaughan Golf Day in Hoylake. It was for the John Moores University Liverpool. He was also hoping to see a few of his old friends in the local area.

Over the following months, Frank had a full list of engagements, not least a special meeting with Luciano Pavarotti at Twickenham on Saturday 19 June. He had been looking forward to these engagements very much, especially the meeting with Pavarotti. He had to cancel his Golf Classic at Hazlemere Golf and Country Club and his meeting with Pavarotti when he felt far too ill to fulfil these commitments.

By now, Frank was getting worse and had a persistent cough, more worrying still there were traces of blood when he coughed. He was sent for tests to try to find the cause of the cough, but nothing was found to be wrong with his lungs. However, when the cough did not clear up, he was admitted into hospital in Oxford for a thorough examination.

It was during this examination that it was found the artery near to his lung was enlarged. He and Stella decided to see their friend and surgeon, Steve Westaby who had operated on Frank some years before. Mr Westaby found that the artery had again torn. However, luckily there appeared to be no problem with his heart. Mr Westaby offered to operate on Frank, and he agreed without hesitation. He had total trust in Mr Westaby; after all, he had saved his life in 1992.

Frank was taken to the John Radcliffe hospital in Oxford for the operation, but it was found that there were further problems. Frank had been on blood thinning tablets, and he lost a lot of blood during the operation. He had to be reopened and closed three times, once in the middle of the night.

Each time this happened, Stella thought he would not survive, but Frank was obviously determined to keep fighting. After the operation, he developed an infection whilst being fed intravenously. He collapsed again, but fought doubly hard. Stella and her sister had spent hours in the visitor's room and eventually Frank began to improve, thanks to his determination, and the skill of the surgeon, and the nursing staff.

He had lost a lot of weight, and was very weak after eleven weeks in intensive care. However, eventually he was allowed to go home. He was very frail, and wandered around the house. He was so used to being busy, and looking towards the next event on his calendar. Frank being Frank, he was probably thinking that if he could get his strength back, he could do a show or two to raise funds for the hospital that had saved his life twice.

He was asking about his sister Phyllis and was about to telephone his other sister, Myra who lived in Leeds, to ask about their sister. At this point, Stella felt she had to tell him herself how ill Phyllis was. Of course, it upset him very much. It seemed that he now was giving up his own fight, as he loved his sister very much. He said it was very unfair as he was the eldest, and that he should be the first to go. Stella comforted him as best she could.

CHAPTER 54

It was Rosh Hashanah, a very important day in the Jewish faith and the week before the fast of Yom Kippur. Stella and Frank held dinner for the family, but Frank could not enjoy it. He was getting weaker and eventually had to leave the table. Stella found him in another room on the telephone to New York speaking to Phyllis's husband. Frank was just devastated and Stella felt he had now completely given up his own fight.

He returned to hospital, but the consultant could find nothing wrong with Frank's heart. He was told to take things easy to help build up his strength.
During the evening, Frank said that he wanted to go home, but Stella could not take him without the consent of the doctors, who were now off duty. She said she would take him home the next morning.

He was still talking about a show to raise funds for the hospital. Stella felt so awful leaving him. She drove home in tears, and went to bed hoping to get him home early next day.

During the early hours of the morning, the hospital called to say that Frank had taken a turn for the worse. Stella woke their son, David, who was staying with them because of the situation with his father. He and his mother drove down the motorway to the hospital. When they were taken in to see him, Frank was unconscious and wearing an oxygen mask. It was such a shock to see him in this condition. Stella was talking to him, hoping he could hear her. She held his hand, telling him that Jamie, their grandson, was asking if his grandfather would go fishing with him. Frank tried to speak, but Stella could not make out what he was saying.

He lost consciousness, and the doctor asked them both to step into a side room. Apparently, it is a belief that when people are so ill, the hearing is the last sense to fade, therefore, doctors do not like to discuss a patient within their hearing. Stella and David were told that a blood clot had been found. David asked what chance his father had, and was told only one percent.

Another doctor who had entered the room asked Stella and David to come back, as Frank's heart was fading fast. Stella held him and told him how much she loved him. It was at this point his heart stopped, and Frank passed away. It was Friday 17 September 1999.

Even though she must have been heart broken at losing Frank, Stella said she was pleased that he had a peaceful end. It was as if he just went to sleep. His wedding ring was removed, and given to Stella. Frank had not removed his ring in forty-eight years of marriage. He had once said his one wish was that he would go before Stella, as he could not live without her. His wish had been granted.

His daughter Susan had to be told of her father's death, so Stella telephoned her from the hospital. As Susan was the only daughter, Frank had made much of her. Naturally, she was totally devastated, she loved her father very much.

On the day he died, their son Andrew was due to open in the leading role in a play in San Francisco but he wanted to fly home immediately. Stella persuaded him not to, and talked him into staying long enough to open the play. There was nothing he could do and he was so far away he may not be home in time for his father's funeral. He decided to stay, and got very good notices in the press but he wanted to go home and be with his family at such a very upsetting time for them all. It was therefore decided to close the play for four nights for Andrew to return home to attended his father's funeral.

Stella had the very upsetting task of arranging the funeral. Frank had died at ten to six on Friday morning. According to the Jewish faith, the funeral should be carried out within twenty-four hours. As this would have been their Sabbath, it could not take place on the Saturday. Decisions had to be made so quickly and it was difficult notifying everyone concerned. There was a lot to organise but fortunately, as Stella's brother in law was a Rabbi, he was able to arrange to lay Frank to rest on the Friday, the day he passed away. Stella was very relieved as they were all very distressed. The family did not want the television, and newspapers involved, which probably would have been the case if the burial had been delayed. Stella contacted Frank's two sisters, who were in Leeds. They both managed to attend, even though it was very short notice.

The funeral took place at three o'clock at Bushey Jewish Cemetery, Hertfordshire.

When the coffin was lowered to rest, the Rabbi placed on top, two heavy bags, each one tied at the top. They were the Siddur, which are very old holy bibles of the Jewish religion. When the bibles become old and dog-eared, new ones are printed but the old bibles are not thrown away because they contain the word of God. When a very eminent, good person, a rabbi or somebody who is held in great esteem dies, they put the Siddur in the grave with them.

The media were informed of Frank's passing immediately after the funeral. The story of Frank's death was reported in every British newspaper on Saturday morning 18 September 1999. Twelve days later, Frank's sister Phyllis also died.

CHAPTER 55

Once the news of Frank's passing was reported, some of the biggest names in the entertainment world wanted to pay tribute to him. Everyone had the greatest respect for Frank, and nothing but good things to say about him.

Tom Jones: "He was a real star. He came from the old school of entertainers - it was to get on stage and entertain, look as good as you could, and sing the way you wanted to sing, but project".

Cliff Richard: "Frankie was a compassionate, kind and generous man. He was the most polished of performers".

Mike Yarwood: "I got to know Frank when I toured with him in the 1960s. Frank was a lovely man. I used to watch him from the wings every night, and think what a great performer he was. As he was one of the performers I used to impersonate, he came to see my act at the Palladium in 1981 - and I could hear him laughing in the audience".

Bruce Forsyth: "It is very, very sad. He will be a great loss to show business; he was a unique entertainer, the likes of which will never be seen again".

The Variety Club's Pip Burley: "We've lost a real showbiz legend, one with a very long and distinguished career. If the fickle finger of fate had pointed differently, he could have become a Hollywood superstar. There aren't many English guys who could say that".

Des O'Connor: "Frankie was one of the nicest people I ever met - a gentleman and a real showman. On stage he was dynamic. Off stage he was a gentleman and a friend, and always ready to help anyone. It is a very sad day, we have lost a wonderful guy. My heart goes out to his lovely wife and family".

Michael Parkinson: "He lived nearby, and I played in his golf tournaments. I also interviewed him once, many years ago. Frank was a very nice man, charitable, funny, affable, great company, and a marvellous all-round entertainer. He was one of the last of a great breed of entertainers. My abiding memory will be of his smile - that big grin whenever you saw him."

Terry Wogan: "He was a simple man who never lost his simplicity or humility. I am very sad and shocked to hear of his death".

Nicholas Parsons: "He was a super guy, a true professional to his fingertips. He worked very hard to polish and hone his work to become one of the outstanding performers of our time".

Sir John Mills: "I was very shocked by Frank's passing as we really thought he would pull through. He had put up such a brave struggle".

Peter Charlesworth: Frank's long time agent and friend said "He was a wonderful, wonderful man and it is a very sad day for all who knew him".

Sun sub-editor Allan Stein: who was an extra in Frank's 1957 film 'These Dangerous Years', said "It was an honour to meet him, he was a legend and a real gent. At the end of our day's filming four or five of us were at a bus stop and he gave us all a lift into London".

When the announcement was made of Frankie Vaughan's passing many people wanted to pay their respects. One such person was Lord Greville Janner. He is a Labour Member of the House of Lords. He was President of the Board of Deputies of British Jews, the main representative body of British Jewry, from 1979 to 1985, and is a key international figure in efforts to seek compensation and restitution of Holocaust victims. He was instrumental in arranging the 1997 London Nazi Looted Gold conference.

Lord Janner said of Frank, "He was not only a great performer. He was a loyal friend, a proud Jew and a man who never refused a mitzvah. His prime charity was the National Association of Boys' clubs. In that role, he awarded and presented the annual "Frankie Vaughan Trophy". From the day in 1955 in the Royal Festival Hall when he handed the trophy to the Brady Ramblers, he became my friend. Frank and Stella came to Leicester to help me get re-elected. From the loudspeaker car , he sang his way through the pouring rain and families came to their windows and waved. Everyone loved him. On or off stage, he was a wonderful man".

Frankie Vaughan was honoured for his charity work last week then he went to Buckingham Palace to receive a CBE from the Prince of Wales.
Said 67 year old Frankie: "Prince Charles asked how my voice was and if I was still gargling with port!"

Frank with two of his fans Barbara and Brian Lees

THE WATER RATS
Bert Weedon, Steve Clark, Jack Seaton, Jimmy Clark, Frankie Vaughan, Not Known.

Frank and Stella.

Frank with daughter Susan and Grandchildren.

Frankie and me at one of his birthday parties at
a hotel in High Wycombe.

Frank and Stella with friends
Pat and Ralph Hassell.

Frank with three Fans at the Night Out,
Birmingham

Jackie Salmons - Fan Club International Secretary

■LIFE SAVING: Surgeon Steve Westaby with the electronic heart and (left) Frankie Vaughan

Frankie's all heart

SINGER Frankie Vaughan helped to raised £750,000 to fund a pioneering project into electric heart transplants which has saved the life of a chronically ill man.

The singer, who has had heart surgery, raised the money with friends to give 64-year-old Abel Goodman a mechanical heart using a new transplant device.

Mr Goodman underwent the operation to implant the artificial device at Oxford's John Radcliffe Hospital after being told he was unsuitable for a heart transplant because of his age and kidney problems.

The operation went ahead last week and today Mr Goodman, from London, was recuperating today despite suffering a slight stroke.

It is the first of what is hoped to be a series of three similar operations funded by the showbusiness star and his friends. They launched a fund-raising campaign a year ago after learning of the pioneering work.

Doctors have hailed the latest surgery as a world first for the modified device.

Steve Westaby, who carried out last week's intricate operation, said around 500 patients had received similar implants in the US but these had been used as an intermediate device for those waiting for human hearts for transplant.

Mr Westaby said the operation had gone extremely smoothly and Mr Goodman was awake just one hour after the implant. The next day he was able to get out of bed and on Friday celebrated his 64th birthday.

Give me the blue plaque: the Heritage Foundation presented a blue plaque to the City of Liverpool, in honour of entertainer Frankie Vaughan, who was born in the city. Pictured (from left): Liverpudlian comedian Tom O'Conner, Mr Vaughan's granddaughter Lillie Marks, his daughter Susan Marks and his widow Stella Vaughan. The plaque is to be mounted at the Albert Dock's Museum of Life PHOTO: MIKE SLADE

Vince Hill wrote the following tribute:

When I first caught the showbiz bug I would have been about 16/17 and was working the clubs and pub s around my home town of Coventry and Frank, I guess, would have been at the beginning of his meteoric rise to super stardom. At that time, I had no big ideas of my own about being a star - just earning few bob at weekends was more than I could ever have hoped for! Finally, I did take the plunge and turn pro and of course came to live in London.

I well remember the first time I saw Frank on stage was at the Chiswick Empire, top of the bill of course, and I was living there then - Chiswick I mean not the Empire! The magic of the man on stage was inspirational and there was I, just starting out and thinking, "Oh boy have I got a long way to go". Although I wanted stardom, it was the impossible dream to me then and never in a million years did I think I would ever meet him. Frank was one of the great gentlemen of the business and having met him on many occasions through the years I know he will always be remembered as such.

They say that what goes around comes around and now I regularly use musicians who played for Frank - and all of them have fond recollections/memories of their time with him. Unfortunately, male singers do not often work together on stage so I only met him socially apart from maybe the odd TV or radio show - very often with his wife Stella, who like my wife Annie, was always 100% behind everything he did. I would love to have known him better. When Frank died, we certainly lost a Grand Master.

Marty Wilde:

In 1957 I joined Phillips records as a recording artiste and my Artists and Repertoire man was a wonderful character called Johnny Franz. Johnny was the main A and R man for Phillips records, and had many hit artistes that he recorded. As a young artiste in my mid teens, I was very much in awe of the many stars that John looked after, and I guess in many ways it was natural that I would inquire about their personalities in case I worked with them in the future. When I asked John about Frank, John would smile and say, "He is a total gentleman and a real pleasure to work with".

This appraisal stayed with me over the years, and when I finally met Frank, I realised how true John's words were. Always courteous and kind to everyone he met; he had a rare charisma that people could feel immediately when they met him. Apart from such great human qualities, he was also a really great artiste who could, and did hold an audience spellbound throughout his great career. I know that Stella played a big part in Frank's life and to meet them both was always a real pleasure, as they were always such a devoted couple.

Finally, we will always miss Frank and be thankful for the good times we had with him.

Sincerely

Marty Wilde

TRIBUTE TO FRANKIE VAUGHAN
By Peter Goodright
(Poet Laureate of the GOWR)

When Young Frankie Ephraim Ableson came south to London Town
He'd no idea of how his skill would bring him world renown
A commercial artist's job, perhaps, would help him to go far
But destiny decreed that Frank would be a Super Star.

A note from Barney Colehan a chance from Billy Mash
Debut at Kingston Empire - where comments could be harsh-
But, what d'you know? They loved him, this new boy stopped the show
He radiated stardom - to the top he would go.

Yes, how the audience loved him. He captured all their hearts
The 'Moonlight' song was introduced releasing Cupid's darts.
The flashing smile, the lidded eyes, 'Is there anyone in doubt'?
There wasn't a girlie watching who wouldn't have loved to try him out.

Transatlantic acclaim - Las Vegas called - International stardom was his
But American values turned out to be not really Frank's sort of show-biz.
Broadway appearances, Hollywood films meant no time at home, that's for sure.
And Frank wasn't keen on being away, spending most of his life on a tour.

He was Deputy Lieutenant of Buckinghamshire, (try fitting that in Rhyme)
And a hero to all the Boys' Clubs to whom he gave much of his time.
To be voted King Rat is an honour - not a thing they decide in a trice
And to show just how much we admired him - we voted him King Rat twice.

Show business is very demanding - not for the faint-hearted to dare
And those who appear in the spotlight need sustenance, loving and care.
For Frank it was Stella who provided these things - through successes,
and sickness and tears.
Her single-minded devotion and love sustaining him all through the years.

So Frank, we're all here 'cos we loved you; Your dear family, and brother Water
Rats too.
Your friends and your fans and your colleagues - You know that we all miss you.
But sorrow is tempered with gladness - for you touched all our lives with your
skill.
And for putting the sparkle in Stardom, you'll always be Top Of The Bill.
Relieved of pain and illness - all earthly cares now cease.
Past King Rat Frankie Vaughan, CBE. May your Dear Soul rest in peace.

Memorial Service
Held on 23 July 2000

Very often, children in their own uncomplicated way, can give expression to profound thought and truth. A story is told about two children who were talking about the death of their father. The little girl asked her brother how their father went to God. "well," said the boy, "it happened this way, first Daddy reached up and up as far as he could. Then God reached down and down, when their hands touched he took him".

Our dear Frank during his lifetime reached up to Heaven in so many ways. He reached up to Heaven with a generous heart, making his liberal contributions to many Jewish and civic causes that were dear to him. He reached up to Heaven with dedicated service and active participation in an impressive number of organisations. But most important of all he reached up to Heaven with a heart overflowing with love for all who were near and dear to him - and God reached down, and has taken him to his divine reward.

He was blessed with a great and generous spirit, lending his name and giving his support to many worthy causes and charitable purposes. He was a source of benefit to men and women, old and young, in all walks of life - That was in this World - A sanctification of god's name. He made millions of people happy with his music and song. He always proudly identified with his people. He was proud to be known as a Jew in the Jewish and non Jewish World. That was also a sanctification of God's name here on Earth.

He celebrated a life of forty-eight years of marriage to his dearest Stella. It was a partnership, as rare and outstanding, as it was legendary, and a shining example to his profession and the wider public. That was also a sanctification of God's name here on earth. He is lovingly remembered by Stella, their children David and Andrew, Susan and husband David, his Grandchildren, his Sisters, Brothers-in-law, Nieces and Nephews and his Mother-in-law Sarah. Frank found grace in the eyes of God, and in the sight of his fellow men. He had a special Soul, and leaves priceless monuments to his memory. These are the good name, as an honourable son of his people, a gentleman, respected and honoured by Royalty and National Leaders and the widest British public, for his benefaction towards others. Adored by millions of loyal fans, and respected by his professional peers. He leaves a memory and presence loved and cherished by a devoted family and friends.

A private Memorial Service for Frank
was held on Sunday 4 February 2001.

It was held at the New West End Synagogue, Bayswater, London. The synagogue minister Rabbi Geoffrey Shisler and Stella's brother-in-law, Rabbi Neville Kesselman, gave the address.

Although they lived in High Wycombe, Stella had chosen this particular synagogue because she wanted a beautiful, Orthodox Synagogue, big enough to accommodate everyone who wanted to go to the memorial. Also, the people who designed the New West End synagogue also designed Liverpool's Princes Road synagogue, where Frank had his bar mitzvah. Among show business people attending the service were singer Val Doonican, lyricist Don Black, and broadcaster Gloria Hunniford. Family and friends were also joined by Lady Grade, widow of the film and TV mogul. It was at Lord
Grade's memorial service that Frank had performed for the last time.

Tributes were read by Mr Michael Harris MBE, Sir Henry Cooper OBE, KSG, and Mr Wyn Calvin MBE, representatives of charities and youth club organisations which Frank supported. Frank's younger son Andrew paid tribute to his father in song, music played by Colin Keyes. Finally, Andrew's older brother David, paid his own moving tribute to their father.

Many people miss Frank's wonderful performances, for which they would travel anywhere in the country. Many of his fans had been members of his fan club since it was founded. They had followed him all over the country and sometimes even overseas too. They were very loyal to Frank, and of course, he was equally loyal to them. He was one Britain's best-loved entertainers of his era.

After his death, it was decided to change the title of his fan club from "Frank and Friends" to "Friends of Frank". It is still in existence today.

CHAPTER 56

It was a very sad time for Stella. When it was all over, maybe she would think back to just over a year previously, when she and Frank had that lovely night at the Savoy, which she had arranged for Frank's birthday. They had enjoyed such a happy evening and danced to "Hello Dolly" and as they left, the band played "Give Me The Moonlight".

Many of Frank's records were played on radio over the following weeks. In addition, The Variety Club of Great Britain held a tribute show on Sunday 12 March 2000. It was at the Empire Theatre, Liverpool, and Frank's own city of birth. It was in aid of The Grand Order of Water Rats, Cardiothoracic Centre, Liverpool.

For a man who left Liverpool with five pounds in his pocket, Frank Ableson achieved incredible things in his lifetime. He made such a difference to the lives of a great number of people. He always felt very lucky for the life he had lived. His wife and family were the entire world to Frank. He had never taken his success for granted, and used to say, "If you take out, you must put something back". Frank certainly did that.

In 2000, Stella donated the complete contents of Frank's music archive to John Moores University Liverpool in the hope that it may be of help to students of music. The collection consists of sheet music, scores, orchestral and band parts used by Frank throughout his career. Many of the scores and band parts have handwritten notes relating to the occasions they were used, including stage directions, lead-ins and running orders for stage and television appearances.

On 22 June 2000, his family and close friends were joined together to attend the consecration of Frank's headstone.

It was inscribed Mr Moonlight - He Enriched Our Lives.

Personal Memories of Frankie Vaughan OBE DL
Jackie Salmons International Secretary
Friends of Frank

Frankie Vaughan was a wonderful entertainer, a true gentleman; he enriched the life of many people including mine. I first met him when I was 18 years of age at the London Palladium, little did I realise then what an influence he, his family and friends would have on me for the next forty yours. I was very privileged to organise Frank and Friends, which his many fans were, he did not like the words fan club. Numerous people, couples and families became his and his family's friends. He had even invited the 'club' to his home for their meeting. He had a wonderful gift of making people, whoever they were, from the drunk at the stage door to the highest in the land, feel special. We saw him and he saw us with young children and then delighting in grandchildren. Many friendships still exist today, we meet up once a year for lunch, and Stella joins us. He left all of us a very special legacy.

He was particularly good with young people and cared passionately about them, hence his many years of supporting the National Association of Boys' Clubs. The work he did for the Easterhouse Project is well documented, he showed the young people he cared. He always said, "We all need to be wanted". I also remember him commenting that we were busy building new cities and town, but there was no infrastructure to accommodate young people, therefore they would get bored, form gangs and get into trouble. Sadly, this now appears to be happening today.

On stage, he loved flirting and teasing through his music with the ladies and making them feel special. He would be thrilled if their partner pushed them forward for attention. A classic example of this was the song for which he was famous "Give me the Moonlight" when he sang 'anyone in doubt,' all the ladies would call 'we are' which would always make him giggle. He always found time to meet people after a show and would spend time talking to them. Again, he always said the most important thing you can give people is time.

I particularly remember being at a variety club tribute dinner in Liverpool, standing at a reception where there were many celebrities and I was feeling a little insecure. The door opened, they announced Frank and Stella, and he walked in, left the mayor, press and dignitaries, walked straight across the room, and gave me a kiss. He introduced me to everyone, instantly making me feel ten feet tall and special!

His wife Stella and his family were very important to him. He was so proud of his children David, Susan and Andrew and what they were achieving with their lives. Then when the grandchildren came along he was over the moon. One of the last concerts he gave was for his granddaughter's school. She rang him up one day and said that her friends and teacher asked her was it true that she had a famous granddad.

Stella was his rock, friend and confidant, they were very much in love, you would always see them after a show walking away together with his arm around her.

The Grand Order of Water Rats, of which he was a proud member and King Rat twice, paid a wonderful tribute to him shortly before he became ill. When he was King Rat, the Water Rats Ball was a fabulous evening when all his show business friends, personal friends and family turned out to support him. It was a very special evening.

A truly great man who certainly 'ENRICHED PEOPLES LIVES'.

Jackie Salmons

Since writing this tribute to Frankie Vaughan, sadly Jackie passed away in 2008.

Tributes from members of the public

Ron Brush - Shard End, Birmingham

As a young man doing my National Service (Royal Signals), I was stationed in Richmond Park, Surrey. On Saturday nights with my mates, we would go into Kingston on Thames. One Saturday night we decided to go to the Kingston Empire Theatre, as there was a variety show on.

During the interval, the manager came on stage to introduce a young singer by the name of Frank Ableson. It was his first time on stage. (Wow! What a voice). I later learned that Frank Ableson was none other than Frankie Vaughan. I felt so privileged to have seen and heard him at the beginning of his successful career.

P.S. He bought the house down!

Janet Boyce - Northfield, Birmingham

My husband's uncle drove Frankie around Birmingham. Uncle's son worked for Philips Records in Digbeth. He told Frankie I had booked a box at the Hippodrome for my 21st Birthday in 1961. Frankie sent me a signed photo and sang to me on the night. (Give Me The Moonlight).

We went to the Night Out after the show but the queue was so long, we came out. Up the road walked Frankie with a bodyguard. I left my husband and friends and just ran and grabbed hold of Frankie. He was so nice. I said to my husband "What a man".

My husband, Tony, has just had Frankie singing Unchained Melody put on his phone!

A Baker - Moseley, Birmingham
I had the great privilege of meeting Frankie on two occasions. The first of them was when I was a young lad with the Moseley Carnegie Boys' Club, to which Frankie was a great ambassador.

The second time being when a friend of mine used to do all the stage props at the Birmingham Hippodrome, and I got to meet Frankie back stage in his dressing room. He had just come off stage ringing of sweat, but still had time for a good chat. I also saw him at the Cresta Club.

Meeting Frankie was truly a memory I will never forget, a true gentleman, so down to earth who never forgot the working class. A man who brought a new dimension to the 50s-60s music. A really great man.

Doris Griffiths - Solihull, West Midlands
I was a waitress at the Cresta nightclub in Lode Lane, Solihull. This was the late 60s or early 70s. I was asked to help Mr Vaughan to change his jackets in between his acts because he was so hot and asked for a mature lady to help him change. I think I was the eldest there, about 40! He was very grateful for the help I gave him.

I was on cloud nine that week, and felt proud to be of help. After the show finished, he asked to see me to have my photograph taken with him. He also signed autographs for all his fans. He gave me flowers and money for the help I had given him.

June Fisher - Sutton Coldfield, Midlands

My father, Harry Hughes, has told the following story many times over the years about Frankie Vaughan: He was in the Junction Public house in Birmingham with several of his work mates, when a tall dark handsome fellow dressed in a white shirt and black trousers walked down the stairs. He proceeded to offer everyone a drink on him. The landlord then pipes up "Do you know it's Frankie Vaughan?" A little old lady sitting in the corner shouts "I'll have a double Frankie". Frank said, "Good on you love, lets make it a treble". The landlord then said to Frank "She has sat in that corner for twenty years drinking only a pint of mild!" Frankie then finished the night by singing 'Cloud Lucky Seven'. He was staring at the Birmingham Hippodrome at the time.

Mrs E Essex - Solihull, Midlands

I remember in the 70s, talking to Frankie Vaughan on the steps of the Cresta Club, Solihull alongside the Ice Rink. He came out for a breath of fresh air, and I was at the ice rink with my daughters who skated there regularly. He was very friendly, I always admired him for the Boys' Clubs he did such good work for. He was a good roll model for the youth of the day, and a lovely man. He is still sadly missed by many people to this day.

Brenda Priest - Hall Green, Birmingham

My brother, Norman King, had quite good connections with Frankie Vaughan as he ran a boys' club for over 50 years altogether. He eventually moved to a club at Court Road, Sparkhill, Birmingahm. Myself, mother and friend, Betty Harris helping out in the canteen. After the death of my mother in 1972, Betty and I continued to help. A few years later, my brother transferred his club to Alcester Road, Moseley, Birmingham. He named the club Asman, as the leader prior to him was Mr Asman. Unfortunately, my brother had to close about two years ago. He was very upset, as Boys' Clubs were his absolute life for a great number of years.

Joyce Toon - Kings Norton, Birmingham

I joined the Frankie Vaughan Fan Club in 1950 due to my brother going out with the Birmingham Club Secretary. One night myself and five friends went to see him at the Night Out Club in Birmingham. My friend Sadie drove us there in her large Humber car. We could not stay to see him after the show, as we had to get home. He was always brilliant in coming out after his shows to greet his fans, and to sign photographs.

We went to get the car to go home and as we were passing the club, who did we see getting into a taxi but Frank and Stella. We all shouted to Sadie to follow that taxi! We sped round an island, tyres screeching. We did not have to go far as the taxi pulled up outside a Chinese restaurant. As they got out of the taxi, we all jumped out of the car and ran to him He said "Where have you all come from?". We told him and he really laughed and was his usual gentlemanly self.

We decided not to hassle him anymore and we kissed him good night, and went home very happy. Show business lost a great entertainer, and his family lost a loving husband, father and grandfather. I am sure all Frank's fans miss him very much, I know I do.

Patricia Roles - Kidderminster

I first met Frank on my twentieth birthday at the Birmingham Hippodrome where he was appearing. He asked anyone with a birthday to come up on stage, so up I went. He sang 'I'm Shy Mary Ellen I'm Shy'. What a lovely evening. In 1973, I was lucky enough to be given two tickets to a tea party at St. Johns Hotel in Solihull. Frank's arm was in a sling at that time, I believe he had been pulled off stage in Derby by an over enthusiastic fan. Before Frank left he had asked me if I would consider being the secretary for the Birmingham area of his Frank and Friends fan club.

When Frank appeared at the Cresta Club, Solihull for two weeks, the headlines in the local newspaper said 'Pack them in Frankie'. It was a full house for the two weeks. He was appearing in Cardiff and as we arrived for the show we all got tangled up with hundreds of rugby supporters who were just leaving an International game.

My most memorable occasion was when Frank and a few of the secretaries from his fan club came to my home for tea. Happy wonderful, wonderful times.

Memories of a Stagehand

I was one of the lucky ones at the Empire Theatre, Liverpool, who met lots of the stars. They were all very nice people, but the one star who stood out as a true gentleman was Frankie Vaughan. I met him when he was staring in Puss in Boots in the 60's.

All the stagehands at the Empire thought the world of Frankie as he treated them as friends. He left me a lovely signed photograph of himself at the end of the pantomime which read, "To Lenny my mate, and I hope that we will always be mates", sincerely Frankie Vaughan. I still have this photograph safe in my album. This time will always remain with me, as he was such a nice person to know.

It wasn't the last time I met Frankie, he came to the Alhambra Theatre, Glasgow, as a stand-in for Harry Secombe, who had taken ill.

The old stage door man told Frankie that there was a Scouser working in the Alhambra and Frankie said, "It's my mate Lenny from the Empire". I was delighted that he remembered me after a couple of years. I have happy memories of this kind and lovely man.

Lenny Johnson - Preston, Lancs

A daughter of the secretary of the Preston branch of "Frank and Friends" wrote the following verse in the late 1950's, her name is Elizabeth. It sums up the relationship between Frank and his Friends.

Fortune be with you, where ever you may go
Guiding you onward, through film-set and show
Reaching you always, where ever you may be
Easing those troubles, which few ever see
Always remember that we are your pals
Shouting and whistling, but good-hearted gals
Never unfaithful right up to the end
Helping you upwards, like any true friend
Kindness and hard work have made you a star
And all of us hope that you'll stay where you are
In singing or acting, we think you're the greatest
As for your records, we all love the latest
Ever with singing we hope you'll go on
For you will be famous, when others have gone.

A while before he passed away, Frank had been interviewed for a magazine article, talking about when he was young. He told how his mother and father had seen very bad times, when they were just married. It was the time of the depression in Liverpool, and his Dad had to go cap in hand looking for work. Frank thought this took away a man's dignity. He said he had always had this fear of having to go through what his father had to, happily, this did not happen. He said he had Stella to thank for that, as she was very good at managing their money. She always encouraged him in his work, supported him in everything he did. She had once bought him a lucky charm, which he always had around his neck. It was a Jewish charm on which was a symbol meaning 'Luck' he was never without it. He always believed in fate and lucky charms.

Frankie Vaughan was a huge star and travelled the world entertaining his fans, but once he was off the stage, he was content with the quiet life. He was not a man for living it up and spending time in nightclubs. He was quite content to be at home with Stella and their children listening to records by the fire. He gave so much to his fans and his audience and deserved the peace and quiet he loved at home.

A great number of people had their lives changed by Frankie Vaughan. He never failed to show interest in, and compassion for the people who deserved help and time, which he gave in abundance.

Personally speaking, I feel privileged to have met him.

Joe Lynch

1950s & 1960s 45rpm UK Discography

1950 The Old Piano Roll Blues / Daddy's Little Girl
1950 Stay With The Happy People / Give Me You
1953 My Sweetie Went Away / Strange
1953 Too Marvellous For Words / No Help Wanted
1953 Look At That Girl / Send My Baby Back To Me
1953 Bye Bye Baby / False Hearted Lover
1953 Hey Joe / So Nice In Your Arms
1953 Istanbul (Not Constantinople)/Cloud Lucky Seven
1954 The Cuff Of My Shirt/Heartless
1954 From The Grape Came The Wine / She Took
1954 Jilted / Do, Do, Do, Do, Do, Do It Again
1954 Out In The Middle of The Night / Crazy About You
1954 My Son, My Son/Cinnamon Sinner
1954 Happy Days and Lonely Nights/Danger Signs
1955 Too Many Heartaches/Unsuspecting Heart
1955 Give Me The Moonlight Give Me The Girl / Tweedle Dee
1955 Wildfire / That's How A Love Song Was Born
1955 Something's Gotta Give / Why Did The Chicken Cross The Road
1955 Seventeen / Meet Me On The Corner
1956 My Boy Flat Top/Stealin'
1956 This Is The Night / Rock Candy Baby
1956 Escape In The Sun / Honey Hair Sugar Lips Eyes of Blue
1956 Lucky Thirteen / Lot's Go Steady
1956 The Green Door/Pity The Poor Man
1957 Garden Of Eden/Priscilla
1957 These Dangerous Years / Isn't It A Lovely Evening
1957 What's Behind That Strange Door/Cold Cold Shoulder
1957 Man On Fire/Wanderin' Eyes
1957 Gotta Have Something In The Bank Frank/single with Kay Sisters
1957 Kisses Sweeter Than Wine/Rock-A-Chicka
1958 We're Not Alone/Can't Get Along Without You
1958 Kewpie Doll/So Many Women
1958 Wonderful Things/Judy
1958 Am I Wasting My Time On You/ So Happy In Love
1959 That's My Doll / Love Is The Sweetest Thing
1959 Honey Bunny Baby / The Lady Is A Square
1959 Give Me The Moonlight/Happy Go Lucky (Re-Issue)

1959	That's My Doll/Love is The Sweetest Thing
1959	Honey Bunny Baby/The Lady Is A Square
1959	Come Softly To Me/Say Something Sweet To Your Sweetheart
1959	The Heart Of A Man/Sometime Somewhere
1959	Walkin' Tall/I Ain't Gonna Lead This Life
1960	What Moore Do You Want/The Very Very Young
1960	Love Me Now / I Was A Fool
1960	Kookie Little Paradise/Mary Lou
1960	Milord/Do You Still Love Me
1961	Tower Of Strength/Rachel
1961	Don't Stop Twist/Red Red Roses
1962	I'm Gonne Clip Yours Wings/Travellin'Man
1962	Hercules/Madeleine
1963	Loop De Loop/There'll Be No Teardrops Tonight
1963	Hey Mama/Brand New Motor
1963	You're The One For Me/I told You So
1964	Alley Alley Oh/Gonne Be A Good Boy Now
1964	Hello Dolly/Long Time No See
1964	Susie Q/I'll Always Be In Love With You
1964	Someone Must Have Hurt You A Lot/Easter Time
1965	The Happy Train/You Darlin' You
1965	Wait/There Goes The Forgotten man
1966	Hurt Yourself/ Nighthawk - with the Valli Boys
1966	Cabaret/Gotta Have You
1967	There Must Be A Way/ You're Nobody Till Somebody Loves You
1967	So Tired/If I Didn't Care
1968	Nevertheless/Girl Talk
1968	Mame/If I Had My Way
1968	Souveneirs/Getting Used To Having You Around
1969	The Same Old Way/You Can't Stop Me Dancing
1969	Hideaway/hold Me Close To You
1970	Peace Brother Peace / You'll Never Walk Alone
1970	With These Hands / I'll Give You Three Guesses
1971	Find Another Love / Lorelei
1971	What Am I To Do With You / Make The Circus Come To Town
1972	Paradise / Same Old Love
1972	Good Old Bad Old Days / The Good Things In Life
1974	Unchained Melody / I'll Never See Julie Again
1975	It's Too Late Now / Somewhere In this World
1975	Close Your Eyes / Our World Of Love

1975	After Loving You / Feelings
1976	I'll Never Smile Again / Ragtime Cowboy Joe
1976	One / Love Is Her To Stay
1977	Red Sails In The Sunset / Seasons For Lovers
1977	Take Me / lemon Drops, Lollipops and Sunbeams
1978	Think Beautiful Things / I Am Lucky
1979	Think Beautiful Things / Simple Kiss
1983	Stockport / Showmanship
1984	Dreamers / Two Different Worlds
1987	When Your Old Wedding Ring Was New / Lucky

EP DISCOGRAPHY

1956   "Seventeen"
Seventeen/Stealin'/Why Did The Chicken Cross The Road? /
Give Me The Moonlight

1956   "Here's Frankie Vaughan"
Honey Hair/Sugar Lips/Eyes Of Blue/This is the Night

1957   "Frankie Vaughan"
The Green Door/Pity The Poor Man/Priscilla/The Garden Of Eden

1957   "Mister Elegant"
Happy Days /My Sweetie Went Away/Look At That Girl/No Help
Wanted

1957   "Swingin' With Frankie Vaughan"
Milord/Green Door/Gotta Have Something In The Bank/Give Me
The Moonlight

1958   "It's Frankie"
Wanderin' Eyes/Man On Fire/Isn's This A Lovely Evening/Single

1958   "Happy Go Lucky"
Happy Go Lucky/Shoe Shine Boy/Lazy River/Bei Mir Bist Due Schoen

1958   "Frankie Vaughan"
So Happy In Love/Wonderful Things/Am I Wasting My Time On
You?/Judy

1959   "The Lady Is A Square"
The Lady Is A Square/Love Is The Sweetest Thing/Honey Bunny
Baby/That's My Doll

1959   "Heart Of A Man"
My Boy Flat Top/Sometime,Somewhere/Walkin' Tall/The Heart Of A Man

1960   "Frank In Films"
These Dangerous Years/Wonderfl Things/The Lady Is A Square/The
Heart Of A Man

1960   "Frankie Vaughan Favourites"
Kookie Little Paradise/May Lou/Milord/Do You Still Love Me

1961   "Let Me Sing And I'm Happy
Let Me Sing And I'm Happy/Cecilia/On Mother Kelly's
Doorstep/Roamin' In The Gloamin'

1961   "Let Me Sing And I'm Happy No. 2"
Ohio/Last Night On The Back Porch/Tiptoe Through The
Tulips/Leaning On A Lamp Post

1961   "Let Me Sing And I'm Happy No. 3"
Broken Doll/Teasing/Ohe, You Beautiful Doll/I will Come Back

1962   "Fabulous Frankie"
Tower Of Strength/Rachel/Don't Stop-Twist/Red Red Roses

ALBUMS

Philips

1958	Frankie Vaughan Show Case
1959	At The London Palladium
1961	Let me Sing - I'm Happy
1961	Warm Feeling
1962	Live at the Talk of the Town
1963	All Over Town
1965	My Kind of Song
1966	Return Date at the Talk of the Town
1967	The Frankie Vaughan Song Book
1971	This is Frankie Vaughan

Columbia

1967	There Must Be a Way
1968	The Second Time Around
1970	Mr Moonlight
1971	Double Exposure
1972	Frankie
1972	Frankie Vaughan Sing-a-Long

Pye

1973	Sincerely Yours
1974	Someone Who Cares
1975	Seasons for Lovers
1977	Golden Hour Presents Frankie Vaughan

Ronco

1977	Frankie Vaughan 100 Golden Greats
1985	Love Hits and High Kicks

Big V Records

1979	Moonlight and Love Songs

FILMOGRPAHY

1956	Ramsbottom Rides Again
1957	These Dangerous Years
1958	Wonderful Things
1959	The Lady is a Square
1959	The Heart of a Man
1960	Let's Make Love
1961	The Right Approach
1963	It's All Over Town

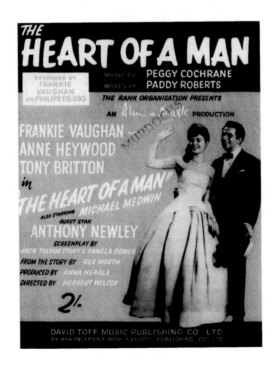

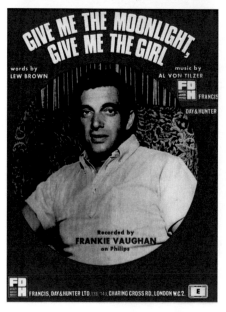

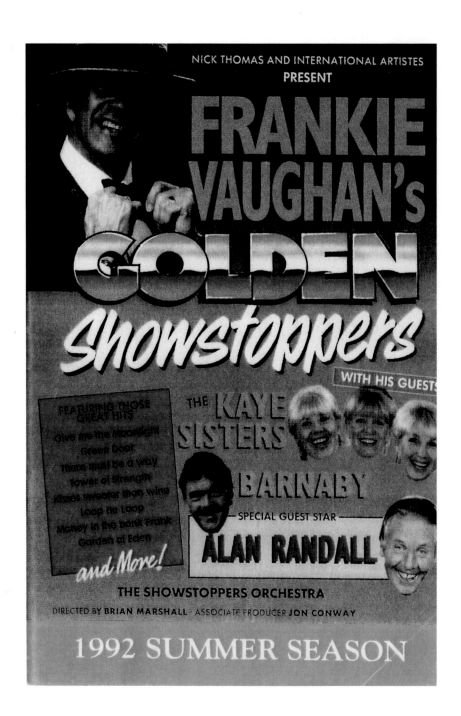

Evenings at 7.30pm Wed & Sat matinees at 2.30pm. **Tickets:** Wed to Sat eves £5.50, £6.50, £7.50, £8.50, £9.50, £10.50 Box: £21.00 Tues ev
and Sat mat £4.50, £5.50, £6.50 Box: £15.00 Wednesday matinee £3.50, £4.50, £5.50 Box: £12.00 **General Concessions:** £2.00 off all abov
ticket prices (excl Sat eve) Family Ticket: 2 children half price with every full paying adult (excl Sat eve) **Party Rates:** (All Perfs excl Sat eve.)
£3.50 off for parties of 50+, £3.00 off for parties of 20+, £2.50 off for parties of 8+ **School Parties:** All seats £3.50 plus 1 in 10 free (excl Sat eve

TRIBUTE SHOW TO
FRANKIE VAUGHAN CBE DL

IN AID OF THE GRAND ORDER OF WATER RATS
CARDIOTHORACIC CENTRE LIVERPOOL

VARIETY CLUB of GREAT BRITAIN

★ at the EMPIRE THEATRE LIVERPOOL

on SUNDAY 12th MARCH 2000 - 7.30 pm

FRANK CARSON - *Host & Compere*

★ FAITH BROWN

★ ROSE MARIE

NORMAN COLLIER ★ JIMMY CRICKET

JOHNNIE CASSON

KEITH HARRIS & ORVILLE ★ LYN PAUL

WYN CALVIN ★ JOHNNIE MORE

JOYCE HOWARD ★ JACK DIAMOND

CEDRIC MONARCH ★ THE ROLY POLY'S

SOUNDS OF BILLY FURY

ABBAGIRLS ★ SEIGE DANCERS

DANNY MANNEX ORCHESTRA

TICKETS PRICED
£20.00 each from the

EMPIRE THEATRE BOX OFFICE.

A SHOW NIGHT NOT TO BE MISSED, GET YOUR TICKETS EARLY

"HITS FROM THE BLITZ III"
Commemorating the 50th Anniversary of the Normandy Landings.

THIS EVENINGS PROGRAMME

5.30pm Pantastics Steel Band.

6.10pm Derbyshire Poet/Writer Douglas Haigh Griffiths reads from his work specially commissioned for this occasion, Freedom and Sacrifice.

6.15pm Parade of Wartime Veterans Associations accompanied by South Notts Hussars RHA Band.

6.35pm approximately, Salute taken by Colonel Sir Peter Hilton K.C.V.O. M.C. K.St.J. Lord Lieutenant of Derbyshire.

6.45pm Display by The Queens Colour Squadron.

7.00pm Evening Concert.

NORMAN WISDOM
In Cabaret supported by Tony Fayne.

• • • • • • • • • • • •

INTERVAL

• • • • • • • • • • • •

ALAN RANDALL:
Will entertain with songs in the George Formby style.

JOAN REGAN:
Will sing a selection of her well known songs including— You Need Me, Smile, When You're Smiling, Ricochet, If I Give my Heart to You, Happy Anniversary, May You Always.

BEVERLEY SISTERS: Singing a selection of their hits, Little Donkey, Once in a While, Rickshaw Boy, The Little Drummer Boy, Sisters.

FRANKIE VAUGHAN: singing a selection of his hits including— Give Me The Moonlight, Green Door, Garden of Eden, There Must Be A Way, Hello Dolly, Cabaret.

• • • • • • • • • • • •

Grand Finale Including
Synchronised Aquatic Show
Supported by Fireworks

• • • • • • • • • • • •

Please remain in your seats until the end of the performance

Celebrating the 50th Anniversary of V.E. Day
Compère: Graham Knight

This Evening's Programme

5.50pm Douglas Haig Griffiths - Derbyshire Poet/Writer reads from his work specially commissioned for this occasion, Adversity Conquered.

6.00pm Marching Display by The Dronfield (Derbyshire) St. John Ambulance Band.

6.15pm Parade of Ex-Service and Civilian Organisations accompanied by The Dronfield (Derbyshire) St. John Ambulance Band. Salute taken by Her Majesty's Lord Lieutenant of Derbyshire Mr John Bather - Concluded by March Past

7.00pm THE BEVERLEY SISTERS

7.30pm CHAS & DAVE

8.00pm Interval

8.15pm THE CHRIS ALLEN ORCHESTRA & SINGERS

8.45pm FRANKIE VAUGHAN

9.25pm Finale

GOODNIGHT

THE BEVS ARE BACK

THE RETURN OF FRANKIE VAUGHAN

FRANKIE VAUGHAN - Singing a selection of his hits including— "Give Me The Moonlight", "Green Door", "Garden of Eden", "There Must Be A Way", "Hello Dolly" and "Cabaret".

CHAS 'N' DAVE - Known for classic songs like "Gertcha", "Rabbit" and "Ain't No Pleasing You".

BEVERLEY SISTERS - Singing a selection of their hits:- "Sisters", "Apple Blossom", "Name", "I'll Be Seeing You".

THE CHRIS ALLEN ORCHESTRA & SINGERS
One of the finest orchestras in Europe, able to delight audiences of all ages with their superb music spanning the years from the 1930's to the present day.

• • • • • • • • • • • •

Please remain in your seats until the end of the performance

GRAND ORDER OF

WATER RATS

Night of the Stars

Annual Ball 1998

KING RAT
FRANKIE VAUGHAN CBE DL

Grosvenor House, London, Sunday 29th November 1998

Peter Charlesworth Limited

2nd Floor
68 Old Brompton Road, London SW7 3LQ

Telephone: 071-581 2478
Facsimile: 071-589 2922

12 October 1992

Mr Joe Lynch
National Schizophrenia Fellowship
9 St. Michaels Court
Victoria Street
West Bromwich
B70 8EZ

Dear Joe

Re: <u>CHARITY SHOW, CHESFORD GRANGE</u>

As of our conversations of last week, it is with deep
regret that I must confirm to you that Frankie Vaughan
will be unable to appear in your charity performance on
25 November 1992. As you have no doubt read in the
papers now, Frank has had a major operation for a split
artery and will be unable to work for at least four
months. I am sure you will understand how he must feel
about this, but there is nothing anybody can do- we all
express our apologies.

Wishing you much luck in the future.

Yours sincerely

Peter Charlesworth

Tom O'Connor

I must be the luckiest entertainer in
the world because, not only was Frankie
Vaughan my mentor, he was also my friend.
All the things I do and all the advice I
give comes from years of watching the master
behave.
A star among stars, nicest guy amongst
all nicest guys, and the most gentle and
charitable person I've ever known.

Page 204

FRANKIE VAUGHAN O.B.E.   16th December, 1991.

Dear Joe and Judy Lynch,

Mr. Vaughan has read your letter and expresses
his sympathy with you in the loss of Simon.

We are sending your letter on to Mr. Vaughan's
agent, Mr. Peter Charlesworth, asking him to
get in touch with you about this.

Yours sincerely,

Barbara Langstone (Mrs)
Personal Secretary to
Frankie Vaughan

FRANKIE VAUGHAN O.B.E.   3rd June, 1992.

Dear Mr. and Mrs. Lynch,

Frankie Vaughan is away at the moment, but
he has seen your letter and he is so pleased
to know that things now seem to be working
out for you.

He and Peter Charlesworth, his Agent, are
glad to have been able to help.

If you manage to get to one of his shows
Please make yourselves known to him.

Yours sincerely,

Barbara Langstone
Personal Secretary to
Frankie Vaughan

FRANKIE VAUGHAN C.B.E.,D.L.

October 1999.

Dear Joe & Judy

My family and I would like to thank you

for your letter and your kind words about

Frank. They are very much appreciated

and have been a great comfort to us all at

this very sad time.

Stella

STELLA

FRANKIE VAUGHAN C.B.E.,D.L.

17th February 1999.

Dear Joe and Judy,

Frank has asked me to thank you for
your letter and for your birthday
wishes. We all missed you at the
birthday bash, but it was a happy day.

Frank was very touched with the poem
by the 8-year old. Thanks for sending
it.

Frank and Stella send best regards.

Sincerely,

Barbara Langstone (Mrs)
Personal Secretary to
Frankie Vaughan